Occurrence Model for Volcanogenic Beryllium Deposits

By Nora K. Foley, Albert H. Hofstra, David A. Lindsey, Robert R. Seal, II, Brian Jaskula, and Nadine M. Piatak

Chapter F of
Mineral Deposit Models for Resource Assessment

Scientific Investigation Report 2010–5070–F

U.S. Department of the Interior
U.S. Geological Survey

U.S. Department of the Interior
KEN SALAZAR, Secretary

U.S. Geological Survey
Marcia K. McNutt, Director

U.S. Geological Survey, Reston, Virginia: 2012

Suggested citation:
Foley, N.K., Hofstra, A.H., Lindsey, D.A., Seal, R.R., II, Jaskula, Brian, and Piatak, N.M., 2012, Occurrence model for volcanogenic beryllium deposits, chap. F of Mineral deposit models for resource assessment: U.S. Geological Survey Scientific Investigations Report 2010–5070–F, 43 p.

Contents

Figures

Tables

Occurrence Model for Volcanogenic Beryllium Deposits

By Nora K. Foley, Albert H. Hofstra, David A. Lindsey, Robert R. Seal, II, Brian Jaskula, and Nadine M. Piatak

Abstract

Current global and domestic mineral resources of beryllium (Be) for industrial uses are dominated by ores produced from deposits of the volcanogenic Be type. Beryllium deposits of this type can form where hydrothermal fluids interact with fluorine and lithophile-element (uranium, thorium, rubidium, lithium, beryllium, cesium, tantalum, rare earth elements, and tin) enriched volcanic rocks that contain a highly reactive lithic component, such as carbonate clasts. Volcanic and hypabyssal high-silica biotite-bearing topaz rhyolite constitutes the most well-recognized igneous suite associated with such Be deposits. The exemplar setting is an extensional tectonic environment, such as that characterized by the Basin and Range Province, where younger topaz-bearing igneous rock sequences overlie older dolomite, quartzite, shale, and limestone sequences. Mined deposits and related mineralized rocks at Spor Mountain, Utah, make up a unique economic deposit of volcanogenic Be having extensive production and proven and probable reserves. Proven reserves in Utah, as reported by the U.S. Geological Survey National Mineral Information Center, total about 15,900 tons of Be that are present in the mineral bertrandite ($Be_4Si_2O_7(OH)_2$). At the type locality for volcanogenic Be, Spor Mountain, the tuffaceous breccias and stratified tuffs that host the Be ore formed as a result of explosive volcanism that brought carbonate and other lithic fragments to the surface through vent structures that cut the underlying dolomitic Paleozoic sedimentary rock sequences. The tuffaceous sediments and lithic clasts are thought to make up phreatomagmatic base surge deposits. Hydrothermal fluids leached Be from volcanic glass in the tuff and redeposited the Be as bertrandite upon reaction of the hydrothermal fluid with carbonate clasts in lithic-rich sections of tuff. The localization of the deposits in tuff above fluorite-mineralized faults in carbonate rocks, together with isotopic evidence for the involvement of magmatic water in an otherwise meteoric water-dominated hydrothermal system, indicate that magmatic volatiles contributed to mineralization. At the type locality, hydrothermal alteration of dolomite clasts formed layered nodules of calcite, opal, fluorite, and bertrandite, the latter occurring finely intergrown with fluorite. Alteration assemblages and elemental enrichments in the tuff and surrounding volcanic rocks include regional diagenetic clays and potassium feldspar and distinctive hydrothermal halos of anomalous fluorine, lithium, molybdenum, niobium, tin, and tantalum, and intense potassium feldspathization with sericite and lithium-smectite in the immediate vicinity of Be ore. Formation of volcanogenic Be deposits is due to the coincidence of multiple factors that include an appropriate Be-bearing source rock, a subjacent pluton that supplied volatiles and heat to drive convection of meteoric groundwater, a depositional site characterized by the intersection of normal faults with permeable tuff below a less permeable cap rock, a fluorine-rich ore fluid that facilitated Be transport (for example, BeF_4^{2-} complex), and the existence of a chemical trap that caused fluorite and bertrandite to precipitate at the former site of carbonate lithic clasts in the tuff.

Introduction

Overview

Current global and domestic mineral resources of beryllium (Be) are dominated by ores produced from volcanogenic Be deposits, and this deposit type can be viewed as a subset of the general class of nonpegmatitic, igneous-associated Be deposits (for example, Barton and Young, 2002 and references therein). Overall, world resources of Be are estimated to be more than 80,000 metric tons (beryl equivalents), and 65 percent of this is in deposits in the United States (fig. 1), primarily from those in volcanogenic Be deposits of western Utah and Be skarn, hydrothermal replacement, and greisen deposits of the Seward Peninsula of Alaska (Alexsandrov, 2010; Sainsbury, 1964), which indicates that the world's current major reserves of Be are nonpegmatitic (Jaskula, 2010). Global production of Be in 2010 was estimated at 190 metric tons Be of which the United States accounted for more than 85 percent. Lesser producers (fig. 1) include China (Changning City, Hunan Province; Fuyun County, Xinjiang Uygur Autonomous Region), Mozambique (Zambezia Province), Madagascar (Ankazobe, Analamanga, Antananarivo Province), and Portugal (Viseu, Centro Region). The Yermakovskoye (Ermakovska) Be deposit in the Siberian Republic of Buryatiya is currently in the development stage with construction of a Be processing plant; the mine is planned to operate at capacity by 2017.

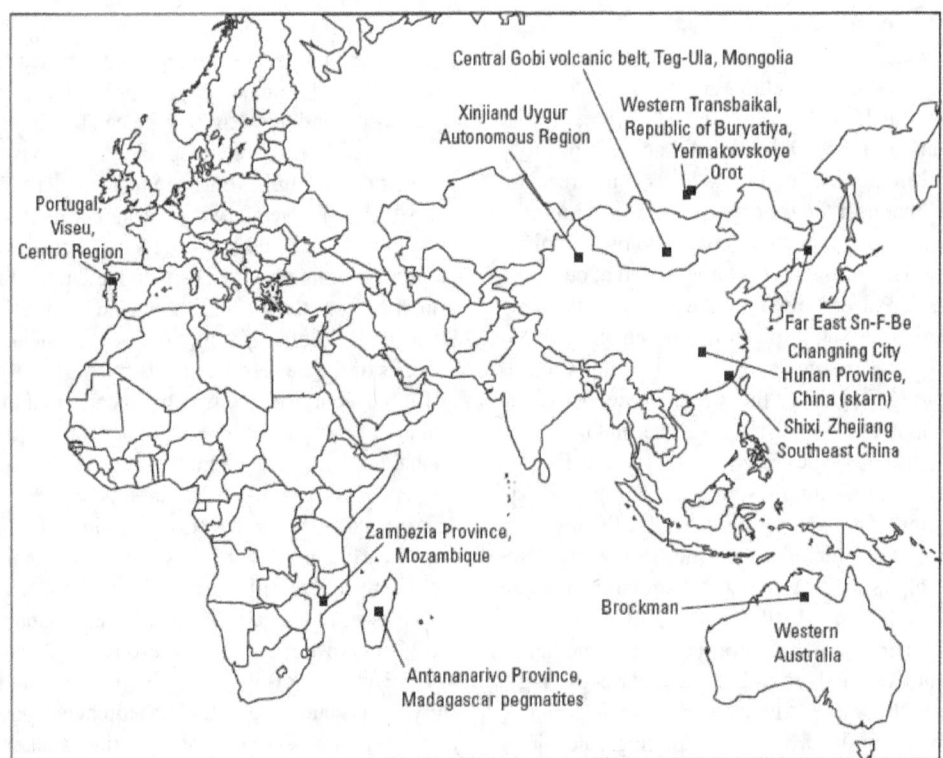

Figure 1.   Map showing the general locations of beryllium resources referred to in the report.

The Be ores constitute the principal global resource of Be for computer, telecommunication, aerospace, defense, and nuclear industries. Beryllium is used to produce light and very strong alloys, metallic glasses, thin foils, and mirrors. Beryllium alloys are used mostly in applications in aerospace, automobile, and computer technologies; oil and gas drilling equipment; musical instruments; medical devices, and telecommunications (for example, Materion Corporation, 2011). Beryllium glasses and foils are used in X-ray imaging and detector applications and Be mirrors are used in satellites and telescope optics and in optical guidance systems. In addition, Be salts are used in fluorescent lamps, X-ray tubes, and as a deoxidizer in bronze metallurgy. The uses of Be in applications for which its properties are crucial are expected to expand rapidly with technological advances (Tomberlin, 2004). For example, if a viable manufacturing process is developed, nuclear fuel containing Be and uranium oxides may prove to be longer lasting, more efficient, and safer than conventional nuclear fuels (Kim, 2010). The cost of Be is high relative to that of other materials, including uranium, and, in some applications, metal matrix or organic composites, high-strength grades of aluminum, pyrolytic graphite, silicon carbide, steel, or titanium may be substituted for Be metal or composites. For example, in some applications copper alloyed with Ni-Si, Sn, Ti, or Sn-P may be substituted for beryllium-copper alloys and aluminum or boron nitride may be substituted for Be oxide, although these substitutions can result in substantially reduced performance.

Scope and Purpose

This report is part of an effort by the U.S. Geological Survey (USGS) to update existing mineral deposit models and to develop new descriptive models for use in upcoming national and regional mineral resource assessments; the models are a necessary component of the current USGS assessment methodology (see for example, Singer and Berger, 2007). This general occurrence model is intended to provide a description of the characteristics of volcanogenic Be deposits, such as those found at Spor Mountain, Utah (fig. 1), which is the dominant resource for domestic Be production. This occurrence model can be used for the identification and assessment of undiscovered Be deposits of this type. The occurrence model highlights the distinctive aspects and features of volcanogenic Be deposits that pertain to the development of assessment criteria and puts forward a baseline analysis of the geoenvironmental consequences of mining deposits of this type. Significant papers upon which the volcanogenic Be deposit model described herein is based include Lindsey and others (1973, 1975), Lindsey (1975, 1977, 1979a,b, 1982, 1998, 2001), Burt and Sheridan (1981, 1982), Christiansen and others (1983, 1984), Ludwig and others (1980), Wood (1992), and Barton and Young (2002). Many of these works build on basic concepts used in categorizing genetic types of Be deposits as discussed in Beus (1966).

Deposits included in this model are economically significant end-members in a group of Be-rich deposit types that form in lithophile-element-enriched volcano-plutonic centers where hydrothermal fluids interact with carbonate rock sequences (fig. 2). To provide a coherent basis for assessing the probability of the occurrence of economic deposits of the type exemplified by deposits at Spor Mountain, Utah, the ore deposit model presented here is restricted in application. This model does not apply to Be skarn, greisen, and replacement deposits that are hosted primarily by carbonate-bearing sedimentary rock sequences intruded by Be-bearing igneous rocks, although they are related by mineralogy and process. Beryllium skarn and greisen deposits, which form by intrusion of granite or rhyolite laccoliths, stocks, or dikes into carbonate rock and concomitant metasomatic replacement processes can have phenakite, bertrandite, and helvite group minerals, and less commonly, bavenite, leucophanite, gadolinite, and milarite (Grew, 2002; Barton and Young, 2002, and references therein). They often display a distinctive texture of rhythmically banded replacements containing alternating light and dark layers of fluorite, Be minerals (helvite-danalite is typical), silicates, and magnetite. Carbonate replacement deposits have distinctly different resource assessment characteristics. Examples of this model include Be deposits of the Seward Peninsula, Alaska.

This model also does not apply to Be deposits hosted by intrusive igneous rocks, for example pegmatite deposits, because those deposits have different petrologic and crystallization histories (Barton and Young, 2002, and references therein). Greater depths of emplacement, higher temperatures, and a source region that constrains the evolution of bulk and melt chemistries result in distinctly different mineralogical attributes and thus economic potential. Well-documented examples of this type have beryl as the primary Be phase.

The format and organization of this report follows a general template designed for use in the USGS mineral resource assessment project that ensures the consistent and systematic inclusion of information related to the occurrence of a broad suite of mineral commodities and deposit models.

Deposit Type and Associated Commodities

Name

Volcanogenic Be type

Synonyms

A number of names have been formally and informally applied to deposits of this type. They include volcanic-hosted epithermal Be, epithermal Be deposits, hydrothermal Be, replacement Be, volcanogenic epithermal Be, Be tuff deposits, and Spor Mountain Be.

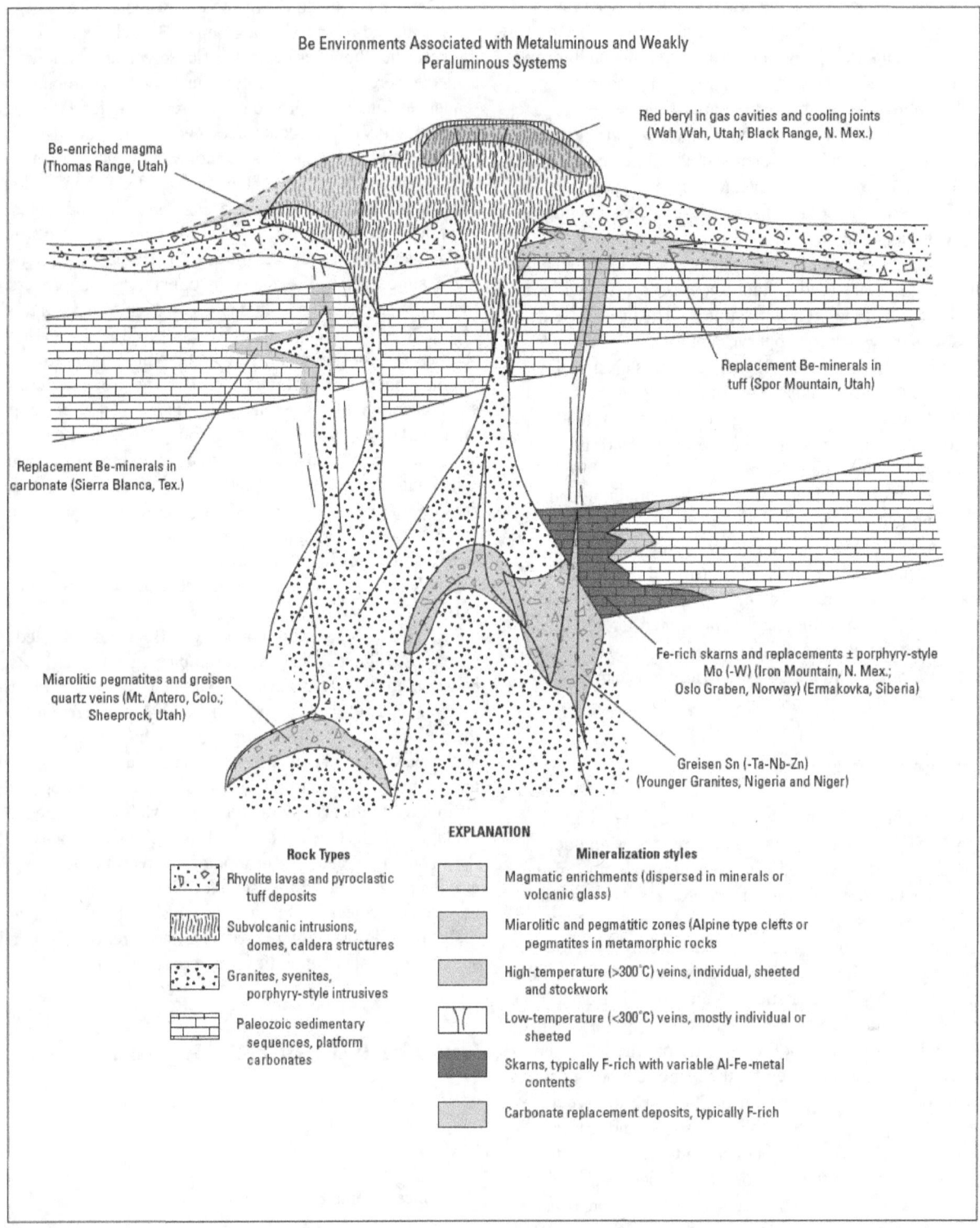

Figure 2. A generalized cross section showing geologic setting and example deposits for the major types of beryllium (Be) resources associated with metaluminous and weakly peraluminous magma systems and the relation of volcanogenic Be deposits such as Spor Mountain, Utah, to other types of Be deposits that are associated with magmas of this general composition. Modified from Barton and Young (2002).

Brief Description

Geological, mineralogical, and geochemical data summarized in this model are intended to be used to aid in identification of tracts of land permissive for the occurrence of volcanogenic epithermal Be deposits, such as those found at Spor Mountain. The deposits at Spor Mountain constitute a globally significant resource of volcanogenic Be (fig. 3) having produced from 1969 to 2009 almost 5,000 metric tons of recovered Be and containing proven and probable reserves in 2009 of ≈10 million tons of ore at a grade of 0.266 weight percent Be (McLemore, 2010a; Brush Engineered Materials, Inc., 2009). For comparison, figure 3 shows grade and tonnage data for volcanogenic Be deposits with selected data for pegmatite deposits, skarns, and carbonate-hosted epithermal deposits. The following description is summarized from Barton and Young (2002) and references therein; original sources are cited in later section.

Volcanogenic Be deposits are hosted by metaluminous to peraluminous rhyolite in which carbonate lithic fragments in tuffaceous volcaniclastic rocks were replaced by fluorite, bertrandite, and other silicate minerals. Deposit origin is primarily the result of igneous processes that lead to the concentration of fluorine and Be in rhyolite melts. Post-magmatic processes also play an important role in the deposits because they cause redistribution and significant localized enrichment of Be to form high-grade ore. These deposits form where hydrothermal fluids interact with lithophile-element-enriched volcanic rocks that contain a highly reactive lithic component, such as carbonate clasts. Host rocks are typically volcanic and subvolcanic (hypabyssal) high-silica biotite-bearing topaz rhyolite and related tuffs and ash flows, although granite porphyry may be present. Together these rocks compose the fluorine-rich igneous suites that are associated with volcanogenic Be deposits. The exemplar setting is an extensional tectonic environment where younger topaz-bearing igneous rock sequences overlie older dolomite, quartzite, shale, and limestone sequences. At the type locality at Spor Mountain, the tuffaceous breccias and stratified tuffs containing Be ore formed as a result of explosive fluorine- and lithophile-rich volcanism that brought ash, carbonate fragments, and other lithics to the surface through vent structures through underlying Paleozoic dolomite rock sequences. The tuffaceous sediments and carbonate lithic clasts make up the volcaniclastic phreatomagmatic base surge deposits. Hydrothermal fluids are thought to have leached Be and other elements from volcanic glass in the tuff and concentrated the Be as bertrandite when the hydrothermal fluid reacted with carbonate in lithic-rich sections of tuff. Hydrothermal alteration of dolomite clasts formed layered nodules of calcite, opal, and fluorite. The principal Be-ore mineral, bertrandite, occurs solely as submicroscopic grains admixed with fluorite. Alteration assemblages and elemental enrichments in the tuff and surrounding volcanic rocks include regional diagenetic clays and potassium (K) feldspar, and, in the vicinity of Be ore, distinctive halos of F, Li, Mo, Nb, Ta, and Sn, and intense potassium feldspathization, sericite, and lithium smectite. The size and grade of a deposit is thought to relate to the distribution of carbonate lithic-rich zones in host tuff and the duration and efficiency of the mineralizing hydrothermal system.

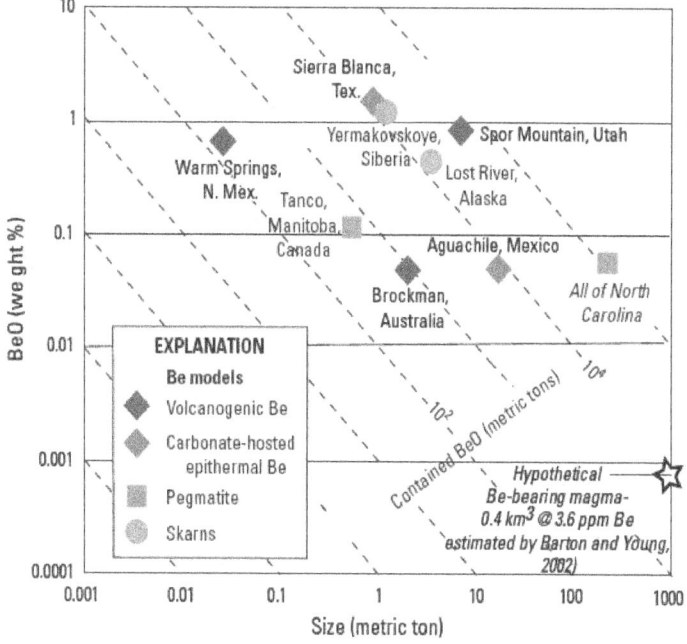

Figure 3. Beryllium oxide (BeO) concentrations (weight percent) and tonnages (Mt, million metric tons) for volcanogenic Be and selected carbonate-hosted epithermal replacement, skarn, and pegmatite deposits. Modified from Barton and Young (2002), McLemore (2010a), and this study. Ppm, parts per million.

Associated Deposit Types

Topaz-bearing rhyolites, such as those associated with volcanogenic Be deposits, are of resource significance for a wide range of additional rare-metal commodities in a variety of deposit types (Kovalenko and Kovalenko, 1976; Kovalenko and others, 1979; Burt and others, 1982; Ludington and Plumlee, 2009; Nash, 2010). Their established economic importance includes (1) volcanogenic deposits of Be, U, Sn, and fluorite, (2) fluorite- and silver-rich base metal ores, and (3) topaz-rich porphyry molybdenum ± tungsten deposits of the Climax and Henderson type (Kamilli and others, in press). Fluorine-rich rhyolites that host volcanogenic Be deposits can also be associated with elevated and potentially economic concentrations of thorium, niobium, and rare earth elements (REE); for example, at the Brockman deposit of Western Australia, the informally named Niobium tuff contains proven reserves of ≈4.3 million metric tons (Mt) of rare metals including 0.44-percent Nb_2O_5 and ≈50–1,500 parts per million (ppm) Be (see table 1 for details and other examples).

Deposit types found in close spatial association with the volcanogenic Be deposits at Spor Mountain include (1) breccia pipe fluorite[1] deposits, (2) carbonate-hosted Be deposits, (3) volcanogenic uranium, and (4) fumarolic gem beryl deposits. These four deposit types are expected to be the most typically associated deposit models for volcanogenic Be. An exception is for fluorine-rich igneous suites dominated by porphyry intrusions or plugs; in such systems Be skarns and greisen deposits containing calc-silicate minerals may also be present. The short descriptions below are compiled from references listed in table 1.

Fluorite Breccia Pipe Deposits

Deposits of fluorite in the Spor Mountain district have been described by Staatz and Osterwald (1959), Staatz and Carr (1964), and Bullock (1981). Commercial fluorite production at Spor Mountain began in 1944 from massive deposits of fluorite occurring as cements in breccias pipes, in veins, and as disseminations that are associated with shattered zones in dolomite at the intersection of faults and vent-related explosive features. The fluorite ore contains 60–90 percent fluorite and is generally uraniferous; a purple color is indicative of uranium. The fluorite mainly occurs as soft powdery masses in dense aphanitic boxwork forms. Unusual forms of purple acicular fluorite with radiating needles in massive fluorite and opaline silica are present in some fluorite pipes suggesting complex replacements of early-formed minerals. These fluorite deposits contain no detectable Be. No fluorite is currently being produced in the Spor Mountain district. At other volcanogenic Be deposits that lack significant carbonate rock, for example the Honey Comb Hills, Utah, deposit, fluorite is

---

[1]These are referred to as fluorspar deposits in older literature. Fluorite is the preferred term for the principal ore of fluorine; fluorspar is considered obsolete (AGI, 2012).

only present as minor replacements as stringers and veinlets in tuff, and as such does not form economic concentrations. In comparison, near the Aguachile carbonate replacement Be deposits of Coahuila, Mexico, sizeable fluorite replacement deposits (≈1 Mt) occur in chimneys, veins, and contact-localized masses in brecciated zones in limestone near rhyolite porphyry dikes. The fluorite is fine-grained, botryoidal, and generally contains less than 20 ppm Be (Kesler, 1977).

Carbonate-Hosted Epithermal Beryllium Deposits

A number of small and irregularly shaped, Be-rich zones are located in carbonate rocks stratigraphically beneath the bedded tuff that hosts volcanogenic Be ores at Spor Mountain. These uneconomic Be occurrences are in Paleozoic sequences of the Sevy Dolomite and Lost Sheep Member of Laketown Dolomite.

More significant carbonate-hosted Be deposits are associated with subvolcanic rhyolite at Aguachile, Mexico, and Sierra Blanca, Tex. The beryllium-fluorine mineralization at Aguachile occurs as replacements and void fillings in brecciated limestone intruded by rhyolite (subvolcanic) porphyry of a peraluminous character (Simkins, 1983; Kesler, 1977; McLemore, 2010a), although the related igneous suite is reportedly peralkaline in bulk composition (McAnulty and others, 1963). Bertrandite is present with calcite and quartz in fluorite-rich deposits in limestone intruded by a rhyolite dike near the ring fault of a caldera, and the principal ore body has approximately 0.3-percent beryllium oxide (BeO) (Kesler, 1977). The igneous rocks provided the bulk of the fluorine, and the limestone provided calcium; deposition was caused by change in pH (Kesler and others, 1983). At Sierra Blanca, western Texas, Be-rich fluorite deposits occur in association with peralkaline-metaluminous volcanic rock sequences. The Be deposits occur within Cretaceous limestones beneath an intrusive contact with an overlying rhyolite laccolith. The rhyolite laccoliths of Sierra Blanca are strongly peraluminous and have anomalous beryllium and fluorine contents (Rubin and others, 1987, 1988, 1990). The alkaline rhyolites are also cryolite-bearing and contain elevated amounts of Be, Li, Nb, Rb, REE, Th, Y, and Zn .

Volcanogenic Uranium Deposits

Deposits of this type form near centers of eruption and more distal as a result of deposition of ash with leachable uranium (Nash, 2010). Hydrothermal fluids remove uranium from uranium-bearing silicic volcanic rocks (typically >10 ppm uranium) and concentrate it at sites of deposition within veins, stockworks, breccias, volcaniclastic rocks, and lacustrine caldera sediments (Breit and Hall, 2011). Immediately east of Spor Mountain, uranium was discovered in 1953 at the Yellow Chief deposit (Bowyer, 1963; Staatz and Carr, 1964; Lindsey, 1978, 1981). Production from 1959 to 1962 was 191 tons of U_3O_8 at 0.20-percent U_3O_8 mainly from beta-uranophane

Table 1. Deposits and occurrences considered in developing the volcanogenic epithermal beryllium (Be) deposit model.

[Data summarized primarily from Barton and Young (2002, their appendix A); Mt, million metric tons; kT, kiloton; Ma, million years ago; ppm, parts per million]

Deposit/ occurrence	Age of complex/ volcanic unit/ mineralization	Brief description of occurrence and contained Be ore	Primary data references
Spor Mountain/ Utah, U.S.A.	Middle Cenozoic/ ≈21 Ma/≈21 Ma and younger	Bertrandite in fluorite-silica replacement of carbonate clasts in lithic tuff (7 Mt at 0.72% BeO), extensive Li-Zn-bearing K-feldspar and clay alteration; overlying 6–7 Ma topaz rhyolites have red beryl	Griffitts, 1964; Shawe, 1966, 1968; Lindsey and others, 1973; Lindsey, 1977; Ludwig and others, 1980; Burt and Sheridan, 1981; Baker and others, 1998
Honey Comb Hills/ Utah, U.S.A.	Middle Cenozoic	Be in fluorite-silica replacements, stringers, veinlets in tuff	Montoya and others, 1964; McAnulty and Levinson, 1962
Wah Wah Mountains/Utah, U.S.A.	Middle Cenozoic/ ≈23 Ma	Topaz rhyolite with late red beryl + kaolinite in fractures with early Mn-Fe oxides; main gem red beryl source	Keith and others, 1994; Thompson and others, 1996
Apache Warm Springs/Socorro County, New Mexico, U.S.A.	Middle Cenozoic/ ≈28 Ma/≈<28– >24.4 Ma, bracketed by stratigraphy	Bertrandite in small quartz veins and stringers in fractures and disseminations in rhyolite and rhyolite ash-flow tuff, intense acid-sulfate alteration	McLemore, 2010a,b and references therein; Shawe, 1966; Hillard, 1969; Be Resources, Inc. at *http://www.beresources. com;* accessed December 10, 2011
Aguachile/ Coahuila, Mexico	Middle Cenozoic/ ≈28 Ma	Bertrandite-adularia-bearing fluorite replacement (17 Mt at 0.1% BeO) adjacent to alkaline rhyolite and riebeckite quartz syenite	Levinson, 1962; McAnulty and others, 1963; Griffitts and Cooley, 1978; Simpkins, 1983
Sierra Blanca/ Texas, U.S.A.	Middle Cenozoic/ 36.2 Ma/coeval with intrusion	Fluorite-rich replacement bodies in limestone adjacent to Li-Be-Zn-Rb-Y-Nb-REE-Th-rich alkaline cryolite-bearing rhyolites; 850 kT at 1.5% BeO as bertrandite, phenakite (behoite, berborite, chrysoberyl); minor grossularitic skarn; clays + analcime	McAnulty and others,1963; Price and others, 1990; Rubin and others, 1987, 1988, 1990; Henry, 1992
Northern Basin and Range Province/ Oregon, Idaho, Nevada, Utah, and California, U.S.A.	Middle Cenozoic/ Miocene	Mainly western Utah Be belt; most occurrences in volcanic rocks, but also skarn (helvite-beryl) and granite-hosted occurrences—dominant Be producer; magmas up to 80 ppm Be	Warner and others, 1959; Shawe, 1966; Lindsey, 1977; Burt and Sheridan, 1986; Congdon and Nash, 1991
Andean Altiplano/ Macusani, Peru	Middle Cenozoic/ Miocene (4.2 Ma; 9.3 Ma)	Beryllium minerals apparently rare, but widespread. Miocene rare-metal-enriched felsic intrusive and volcanic centers, many with Sn-Ag-(±B) ores, fluorite is relatively uncommon; Macusani tuff	Pichavant and others, 1988a,b; Lehmann and others, 1990; Dietrich and others, 2000; Noble and others, 1984
Transbaikal/ eastern Mongolia Teg-Ula	Mesozoic	Many deposit types associated with mainly Mesozoic granitoids ranging from peraluminous to peralkaline; volcanic-hosted Be in Mongolia	Kovalenko and Yarmolyuk 1995; Kremenetsky and others, 2000; Reyf and Ishkov, 2006; Lykhin and others, 2010
Shixi/ Zhejiang, South China	Mesozoic?	Hypabyssal dikes of porphyritic sodic rhyolite, albitized and sercitized, high Be (as helvite, beryl, bertrandite, and euclase) and Nb, Ta, Zr, F	Lin, 1985
Brockman/Western Australia	Paleoproterozoic/ 1870 Ma	Hydrothermally altered fluorite-bearing alkali rhyolite with Nb-Zr-REE-Ta-Be enrichment (4.3 Mt at 0.08% BeO); predates orogenesis	Ramsden and others, 1993; Taylor and others, 1995a,b

$(Ca(UO_2)_2(SiO_3OH)_2 5H_2O)$ occurring in bed-parallel lenses in volcanic sandstone and conglomerate that directly underlie 21-Ma tuff and rhyolite. At the Yellow Chief mine, secondary uranium minerals make up tabular lenses of ore in the tuffaceous rocks. A small amount of uranium was also produced (no data reported) from the Apache Warm Springs, N. Mex., deposit (Hillard, 1969).

Gem Beryl Deposits

Rare gem-quality red beryl occurs in miarolitic cavities in topaz rhyolite (Keith and others, 1994; Thompson and others, 1996; and Christiansen and others,1997). Such gem deposits are likely to occur in vesicular lavas found in volcanogenic Be environments. At Spor Mountain, the strongly colored manganese-rich beryl is restricted in occurrence to vesicles in the young topaz rhyolites that overlie the rhyolites that contain the Be ores and occurs in association with kaolinite, topaz, bixbyite, quartz, and manganese-iron oxides. At Wah Wah Mountains, Utah, occurrences of late-forming red beryl, clay minerals (primarily kaolin and mixed-layer clays), and

manganese-iron oxides are present in fractures in ≈23-Ma topaz rhyolite. The small amounts of beryl associated with fractures in these volcanic rocks are thought to have formed by local redistribution of Be leached from host topaz rhyolites.

Beryllium-Fluorine Skarn-Greisen Deposits

Fluorine-beryllium deposits associated with tin deposits, for example those of the Seward Peninsula, Alaska (Sainsbury, 1964; Alexsandrov, 2010), and the Russia Far East (Rodionov, 2000), are localized in the contact aureoles of carbonate rocks intruded by high-silicon (leucocratic), fluorine-rich granites. The Be is contained in veins and vugs in fluoritized and calc-silicate altered limestone and argillized granite. Beryl, helvite group minerals, and phenakite occur along with quartz, fluorite, topaz, tourmaline, zinnwaldite and other micas, calcite, garnet, and sulfide minerals. Beryllium-fluorine skarn and greisen deposits of this type are analogs of volcanogenic Be that form in deep, high-pressure environments, and where present, may represent the roots of volcanogenic Be systems (fig. 4).

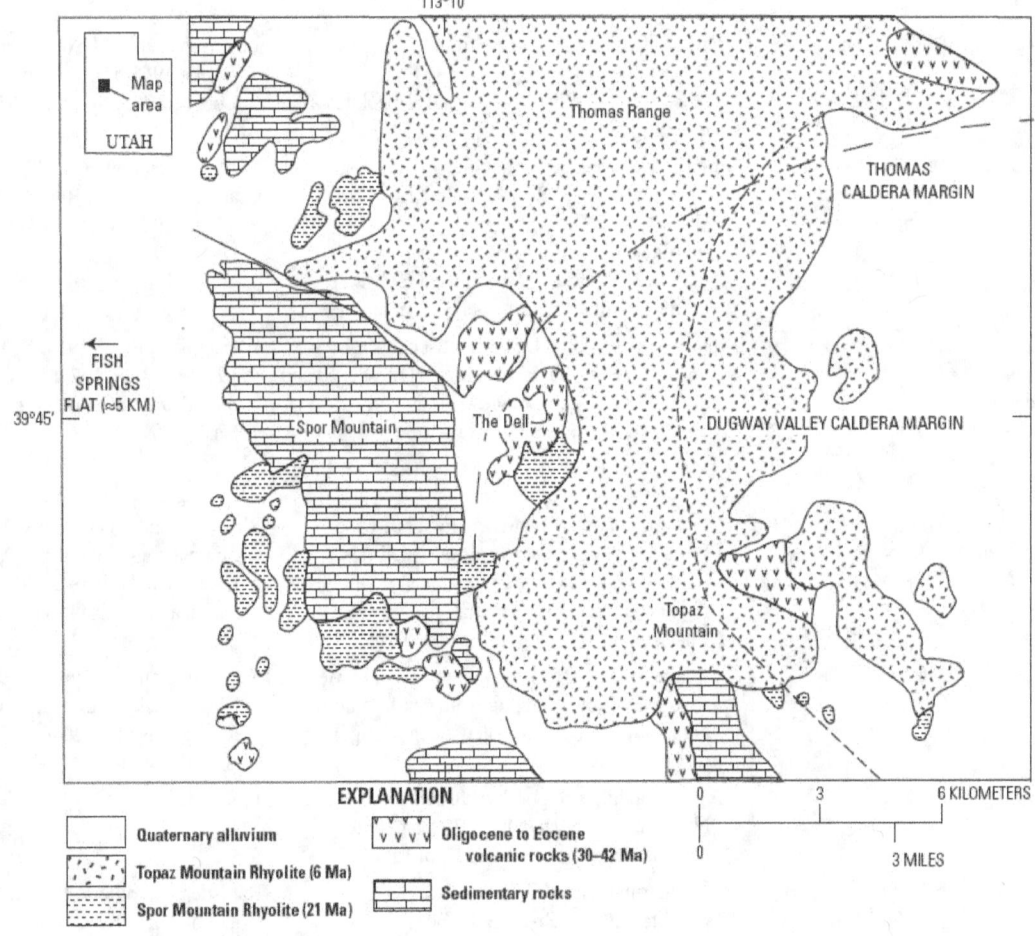

Figure 4.   Generalized index map showing locations of features of the Thomas Range, Utah, as referred to in the report.

Primary and Byproduct Commodities

The sole commodity produced at mines of the Spor Mountain district is Be, and it is chiefly present as bertrandite, although Be-bearing smectites (saponite) also occur in the deposits. The ores at Spor Mountain average less than 1-percent BeO and are economically competitive with higher grade beryl deposits because the volcanogenic ores are minable by open-pit methods and can be extracted by acid-leaching (Lindsey, 1977). Fluorite, uranium, and gem beryl have been produced in former operations at mines in the Spor Mountain district, generally as principal commodities rather than as byproducts of Be mining. Volcanogenic rare metal deposits at Brockman in Western Australia and elsewhere (see table 1) are known to contain enrichments of Nb, REE, Ta, and Zr in addition to Be. The metals could potentially be mined as either byproducts (REE, Be) or primary commodities (niobium), although none are currently being produced at that deposit or at any others.

The BeO grades and tonnages for known volcanogenic Be-bearing mineral deposits are shown in figure 3 along with comparative data for Be deposits that are hosted by carbonate sequences or pegmatites. The estimates as compiled by Barton and Young (2002) and McLemore (2010a) are derived from published resource estimates and geologic inventories that reflect the sparse available data.

Example Deposits

All currently recognized volcanogenic Be deposits and Be-rich tuffs are listed in table 1, and their general locations are shown on figure 1. Only a limited number of deposits of volcanogenic Be are known globally and only deposits of the Spor Mountain district have been studied in detail. The deposit-model attributes described below are based primarily on published studies of current and formerly active mine sites at Spor Mountain, which include North End, Taurus, Monitor, Roadside, Rainbow, Blue Chalk, Hogsback, and Claybank mines (Lindsey and others, 1973, 1975; Lindsey, 1975, 1977, 1979a, 1982, 1998, 2001). Similar, although smaller, domestic occurrences of Be minerals in tuff are present in the Honey Comb Hills, about 30 km west of Spor Mountain (Montoya and others, 1964; McAnulty and Levinson, 1964) and at Apache Warm Springs, N. Mex. (McLemore, 2010a,b).

Beryllium-bearing tuffaceous rocks that have a potential to host volcanogenic Be deposits occur in a number of regions world-wide (table 1). Beryllium tuffs of Mongolia (Kovalenko and Yarmolyuk, 1995), such as those that occur at Teg-Ula within the central Gobi volcanic belt, average 500 ppm Be, and their geochemical and mineralogical characteristics resemble those of Be tuff at Honey Comb Hills and low grade ores of Spor Mountain. The Mongolian tuffs contain clasts of rhyolite, ongorhyolite (sodium-rich), and fluorite and are only weakly kaolinitized or unaltered. However, they are devoid of the fluorite-opal nodules that are greatly enriched

in Be at Spor Mountain. Beryllium-bearing ashflow tuffs also occur in the Macusani region of southeastern Peru (Noble and others, 1984). The highly peraluminous rocks that compose the Neogene Macusani volcanic field may be a northernmost expression of the Bolivian tin belt. The tuffs contain elevated concentrations of Be ($\approx$15–37 ppm) and other lithophile elements and host small occurrences of uranium and base- and (or) precious-metal-bearing minerals, but no known Be deposits.

At the Brockman deposit in the Pilbara region of Western Australia (Ramsden and others, 1993), a niobium-rich ash-flow tuff, informally referred to as the Niobium tuff, contains bertrandite with fluorite in late-stage calcite veins and Be is anomalously enriched (50–1,500 ppm Be) throughout the K-feldspar and quartz matrix. The Brockman deposit primarily consists of low-grade lenses of Zr-Nb-Ta-REE mineralization. The mineralization is associated with the pyroclastic eruption of a Paleoproterozoic trachytic magma enriched in volatiles and incompatible elements. Trace gadolinite ($Be_2FeY_2Si_2O_{10}$) also occurs in trachyte flows that ovelie the Niobium tuff.

Deposits and occurrences of Be in Mongolia and Siberia, Russia, reportedly are hosted by fluorine-rich igneous suites such as those typically associated with volcanogenic Be deposits (volcanic and subvolcanic high-silica biotite-bearing topaz rhyolite and granite porphyry) (fig. 2). Although most of these deposits are hosted by granites (or subvolcanic porphyry) and likely formed at greater pressures or depths than tuff-related Be deposits (for example, Zabolotnaya, 1977; Reyf, 2008; and references therein) (fig. 2), some of them have bertrandite instead of topaz, phenakite, or beryl as the principal Be-mineral. Therefore, there may be the potential for volcanogenic Be in shallowly emplaced portions of these igneous suites. For example, in Mongolia, the central Gobi volcanic zone contains volcanic ongonite (topaz-bearing rhyolite), Be-rich tuff, and REE-rich alkaline volcano-plutonic rocks that compose part of a late Mesozoic rare metal metallogenic belt within the Transbaikal-Mongolian rare-metal province. However, most Siberian occurrences are hosted by Mesozoic granitoid and subvolcanic rocks and formed at greater depths as carbonate replacement or skarn-greisen deposits (fig. 2). For example, the Yermakovskoye fluorine-beryllium deposit occurs in a large carbonate block ("roof sag") within a carbonate-terrigenous sequence preserved in a field of a pre-Mesozoic gabbroic complex intruded by younger Mesozoic alkali granite and leucogranite. The phenakite-microcline-fluorite ores formed at $\approx$224 Ma by replacement of the shattered limestone (Lykhin and others, 2010) and have an average grade of 1.5-percent BeO (Reyf, 2008). Another example is the Orot bertrandite deposit—a large low-grade deposit associated with alkaline granitoids of the Malokunalei complex and volcanic rocks of the Orot paleovolcano (Reyf and others, 2006; Lykhin and others, 2004). The age of the Orot volcanic edifice is 236.4 Ma and the age of granitoids (granite or hypabyssal rhyolite) of the Malokunalei complex, which host mineralization, is 224.8 Ma (Lykhin and others, 2004). The Western Transbaikalian beryllium metallogenic province and all known Be deposits and occurrences are thought to be related to intracontinental rifting. The ores consist of veinlets and replacements of dickite and bertrandite; the ore grade is ≈3,500 ppm BeO.

Metallogenic Provinces and Epochs

The global occurrence of Be-bearing tuff is generally not restricted in age or epoch, as various deposits and potential host rocks range in age from Paleoproterozoic to late Miocene (table 1). Known domestic deposits and occurrences of the class are restricted in age to topaz-bearing Tertiary-age rocks of the Deep Creek-Tintic belt, of western Utah (Shawe, 1972), the Trans-Pecos region of Texas (Rubin and others, 1987), and southern New Mexico (McLemore, 2010a). Barton and Young (2002) provide a comprehensive examination of documented nonpegmatitic Be deposits and Be-bearing belts found worldwide. Globally, rare metal metallogenic provinces favorable for volcanogenic Be deposits are restricted to a small number of locations (table 1, fig. 1) where Be-bearing rhyolite or volcanic ongonite have been identified. These include Brockman, Western Australia; Macusani, Peru; Teg-Ula, Mongolia; and Shixi, Zhejiang, South China.

Historical Evolution of Descriptive and Genetic Knowledge and Concepts

Barton and Young (2002) present a general classification system for the occurrence of igneous-associated Be deposits that is based on the significant known nonpegmatitic Be deposits and occurrences, the petrologic setting and geochemical nature of associated igneous rocks, compositional variations of intruded rock sequences, and potential metasomatic or hydrothermal enhancement processes. Using their classification system, the Spor Mountain deposits are of the rhyolite-metasomatic-carbonate-replacement type. Aspects of the classification system of Barton and Young (2002) that illustrate this particular deposit model and the continuum that exists among the distinct styles of mineralization are summarized in table 2. The generalized geologic setting for the volcanogenic Be assessment model and related Be-deposit models is portrayed in figure 2.

The current descriptive knowledge and genetic concepts relevant to volcanogenic epithermal Be deposits support a volcanogenic origin for metals in the host tuffs and an epithermal origin for subsequent reconcentration into ore-grade material. The Spor Mountain, Utah, Be deposits were discovered in

Table 2. Types of nonpegmatitic beryllium (Be) occurrences (from Barton and Young, 2002, with modifications from McLemore, 2010a, and references both therein, unless otherwise noted). The rhyolite-carbonate type includes deposits of the volcanogenic Be and carbonate-replacement Be models.

[1. Lists main Be-bearing phases; 2. Example localities]

		Igneous	Metasomatic	
Type	**Variety**	**Magmatic**	**Aluminosilicate (greisen, vein)**	**Carbonate (skarn, replacement)**
Granite	metaluminous to peraluminous	1. Lithium micas, beryl 2. Beauvoir, France; Sheeprock, Utah, U.S.A.; Pikes Peak batholith, Mt. Antero, Colo., U.S.A.; Redskin Granite, Colo., U.S.A.	1. Beryl, phenakite 2. Sherlova Gora, Russia; Mt. Antero, Colo., U.S.A.; Boomer mine Colo.; Aqshatau, Kazakhstan	1. Phenakite, chrysoberyl, bertrandite, helvite group 2. Lost River, Alaska, U.S.A.; Mt. Wheeler, Nev., U.S.A.; Mt. Bischoff, Australia; Victorio Mts., N. Mex., U.S.A. (Donahue, 2002)
Rhyolite	metaluminous to peraluminous	1. Be in glass or micas 2. Macusani, Peru; Topaz rhyolites, Western U.S.A. (for example, Thomas Range, Utah)	1. Beryl 2. Wah Wah Mtns., Utah, U.S.A.; Black Range, N. Mex., U.S.A. (compare Spor Mtn., Utah	1. Bertrandite 2. Spor Mtn., Utah, U.S.A.; Aguachile, Mexico (Simpkins, 1983); Sierra Blanca, Tex., U.S.A.; Iron Mountain, N. Mex., U.S.A. (Nkambule, 1988)

The Association header spans "Type" and "Variety"; the Metasomatic header spans "Aluminosilicate (greisen, vein)" and "Carbonate (skarn, replacement)".

1959 using exploration methods that combined the recognition that Be was associated with highly evolved felsic rocks and fluorine-rich hydrothermal systems (Griffitts, 1965; Shawe, 1966) and the availability of a neutron-sourced gamma ray spectrometer capable of rapid semiquantitative field analysis of the Be contents of rocks (for example, Meeves 1966). Most early exploration and assessment models for volcanogenic Be were based on identifying Be-bearing tuffs that provided the correct geochemical signature for such ore and local and regional alteration patterns that might target economic mineralization (Lindsey, 1977). Recognition of textures indicative of phreatomagmatic base surge deposits (Burt and Sheridan, 1986) was a critical factor in understanding the genesis of the ore zones at Spor Mountain because the highly reactive dolomite fragments in the tuff were important to localization of high-grade ore. Studies by Ludwig and others (1980) established the presence, timing, and duration of a long-lived hydrothermal system that is implicated in ore formation. Mineralizing processes involving both ascending magmatic-hydrothermal fluids and circulating meteoric groundwater have been proposed to explain the origin of these Be deposits.

Regional Environment

Geotectonic Environment

Volcanogenic Be deposits are predicted to form where there are magmatic and sedimentary source rocks of a permissive composition. The exemplar setting is an extensional tectonic environment, such as that characterized by the Basin and Range Province of the Western United States. During the late Cenozoic, extensive regions of western North America experienced bimodal volcanism that produced suites of basalt and rhyolite rocks related to development of the Basin and Range Province, including topaz-bearing igneous rock sequences that intrude and overlie older carbonate-dominated sequences of dolomite, quartzite, shale, and limestone (Christiansen and Lipman, 1972). In the Western United States, topaz rhyolites ranging in age from 50 Ma to as young as 0.06 Ma are known to occur in as many as 30 distinct eruptive centers that formed during periods of regional extension, lithospheric thinning, and high heat flow (Christiansen and others, 2007, and references therein).

Topaz rhyolites associated with this deposit type have been studied extensively in the Western United States (Christiansen and others, 1983, 1984, 1986, 1988). They are thought to be extrusive equivalents of anorogenic (A-type) or residual (R-type) granitoid bodies based on their occurrence in an extensional tectonic setting and distinctive geochemical characteristics (Burt and others, 1982; Christiansen and others, 1983). In both bulk composition and mineralogy, topaz rhyolites are thought to be similar to evolved parts of rapakivi granite complexes, such as the Proterozoic complexes of southern Finland and Latvia (Christiansen and others, 2007). Geochemical attributes of anorogenic granites are compared to those of topaz rhyolite in table 3. Both rock types are elevated in REE (particularly heavy REE in the case of topaz rhyolite) and in rare metals including Nb, Ta, Sn, Zr, and Y, and in F and Cl. Burt and others (1982) attribute their petrogenesis to partial melting of older continental crust in a high heat-flow regime, which has the effect of enriching fluorine over H_2O in minerals. Related mafic magmas are thought to provide the heat for melting and further differentiation is suggested

Table 3. Geochemical comparison of anorogenic granites and topaz rhyolites (from Burt and others, 1982; Christiansen and others, 2007).

Feature	Anorogenic (A-type) granite[1]	Topaz rhyolite
f_{H2O}	Low	Low
HF/H_2O	High	High
f_{O2}	Low to moderate	Low to moderate (near QFM)
T	High	Low to moderate (600–800°C)
SiO_2	High ($\approx$76%)	High (73–78%)
Na_2O	High	Moderate-high (3–4.5%)
CaO	Low	Low (<0.8%)
REE	High, except Eu	Moderate LREE, high HREE, low Eu
Enriched	Ga, Nb, Sn, Ta, Y, Zr	Ga, Li, Nb, Rb, Sn, Ta, Th, U, Y
Depleted	Ba, Co, Cr, Eu, Ni, Sc, Sr	Ba, Co, Cr, Eu, Sc, Sr, Zr
F and Cl	High	High; F (0.3–1.5%) Cl (700–1,700 ppm)
Fe/Fe + Mg	High	High
K_2O/Na_2O	High	Moderate to high

[1]After Loiselle and Wones (1979), Wones (1979), and Eby (1992).

to depend upon a variety of factors including (1) zone refining during ascent, (2) extreme fractional crystallization, (3) dehydration due to early pyroclastic volcanism, and (4) apical enrichment of near-surface magma chambers due to liquid-state processes (Burt and others, 1982). More recently, Christiansen and others (2007) proposed that rather than being the melt product of midcrustal granodiorites or being derived solely from felsic crust that either was previously dehydrated or previously had melt extracted (as had been previously suggested), the topaz rhyolites formed by fractional crystallization of silica magmas. The silica magmas originated by small degrees of melting of hybridized continental crust containing a significant juvenile mantle component that was probably derived from within-plate mafic intrusions. Christiansen and others (2007) further note that the mafic mantle-derived magma probably formed by decompression related to the lithospheric extension or, perhaps, convection flow driven by the foundering of a subducting lithospheric plate.

The volume of topaz rhyolite typically erupted from a single volcanic vent in the Western Unites States is generally less than 10 km^3; for example, the volume of the topaz rhyolite at Honey Comb Hills in west-central Utah is 1.5 km^3. Larger volumes of coalesced domes and magmas (as much as 50 km^3) are known at Wah Wah Mountains and in the Thomas Range in Utah (Christiansen and others, 1986) and in the Black Range of New Mexico (Duffield and Dalrymple, 1990). An important example is the Topaz Mountain Rhyolite, which caps the Be-ore-bearing tuffs and lavas of the Spor Mountain Formation (fig. 4). The felsic unit has an estimated minimum volume of 50 km^3 (Turley and Nash, 1980) and is thought to have erupted from at least 12 distinct vent structures (Lindsey, 1979b).

Geologic Setting of Spor Mountain Deposits

Beryllium deposits of the Spor Mountain district (fig. 5) are situated mainly along the western side of the ring fracture of the Thomas caldera (fig. 4). The Thomas caldera was one of a group of at least three Oligocene volcanic subsidence structures that together form an east- to west-trending belt of igneous rocks and related mineral deposits referred to as the "Be belt of western Utah."

The Thomas Range consists of three groups of volcanic rocks that overlie a Paleozoic sedimentary sequence near Spor Mountain (fig. 4), which is an uplifted block of multiple faulted Paleozoic sedimentary rocks bounded on the east by Basin and Range faulting (Lindsey, 1977; Lindsey, 1979a,b; Lindsey and others, 1975; Shawe, 1972). The oldest group of volcanic rocks consists mainly of latitic, andesitic, and basaltic flows and agglomerates of late Eocene age that are exposed along the east side of the Thomas Range. These 42–39 Ma lava flows, breccias, and tufs of rhyodacite to quartz latite composition were erupted from small central volcanoes and possibly from fissures, culminating in eruption of the Mount Laird Tuff and collapse of the Thomas caldera. Copper, gold, and manganese mineralization accompanied the Thomas caldera cycle. The middle group of volcanic rocks consists of Oligocene ash-flow tuffs of quartz latite and rhyolite compositions that are well exposed in The Dell (fig. 4), an area of ash-flow tuff that separates the Spor Mountain block from the Thomas Range and has been interpreted as a caldera ring fracture (Shawe, 1972). Eruption of rhyolitic Joy Tuff at 38–37 Ma was accompanied by collapse of the Dugway Valley caldera and followed by eruption of Dell Tuff at 32 Ma. No mineralization was associated with formation of the Dugway Valley caldera.

The youngest group of volcanic rocks of the Thomas Range (fig. 4; table 4) consists of alkali rhyolite tuff and flows of the Spor Mountain Formation, which erupted at approximately 21 Ma, and the Topaz Mountain Rhyolite, which formed at 7–6 Ma accompanying Basin and Range block faulting (Lindsey, 1979a). The Spor Mountain Formation consists of two informal members: the lower beryllium tuff member and an upper rhyolite lava flow member (figs. 5B and 5C; 6A and 6B). Sanidine from the beryllium tuff member has an age of 21.73±0.19 Ma (Adams and other, 2009). Most of the Be mineralization at Spor Mountain is contained in the beryllium tuff member (Staatz, 1963), which includes tuffaceous breccia, stratified glassy tuff with clasts of sedimentary and volcanic rocks, and thin beds of ash-flow tuff, bentonite, and epiclastic tuffaceous sandstone and conglomerate (figs. 6A and 6B). The tuffaceous breccia and stratified tuff dominate the section near the Be deposits but give way to bentonite and tuffaceous sandstone and conglomerate laterally to the north and east (Lindsey, 1979b). The breccias consist of lithic fragments with abundant coarse, angular carbonate clasts (fig. 6C); the breccias are unsorted, laminar, and cross bedded with bomb sags. They are interpreted as phreatomagmatic base surge deposits because they are positioned beneath a rhyolite dome complex next to known volcanic vents (Burt and others, 1982; Christiansen and others, 1986). The overlying rhyolite lava flow member of the Spor Mountain Formation (fig. 6B) consists of relatively impermeable rocks enriched in fluorine and beryllium (table 4). The younger lava flows and tuffaceous units of the Topaz Mountain Formation form an extensive (>150 km^2), partially dissected plateau atop the Spor Mountain Formation (fig. 4).

The chemical compositions of the Spor Mountain Formation and Topaz Mountain Rhyolite are shown in table 4. Analyses of melt inclusions show that the concentrations of beryllium and fluorine in quartz phenocrysts in Spor Mountain beryllium tuff and a crosscutting 21.56-Ma intrusive plug are indistinguishable, ranging from below detection to ≈1.4 weight percent fluorine and from below detection to ≈108 ppm beryllium (fig. 7) (Adams and others, 2009). These values are similar to whole rock analyses of vitrophyre in the tuff and flow (Christiansen and others, 1983, 1984; Webster and others, 1989). Thus, the median Be concentration of the melt (59 ppm, fig. 7) is about eight times that of the clinoptilolite-potassium feldspar altered vitric tuff (7 ppm Be, table 4).

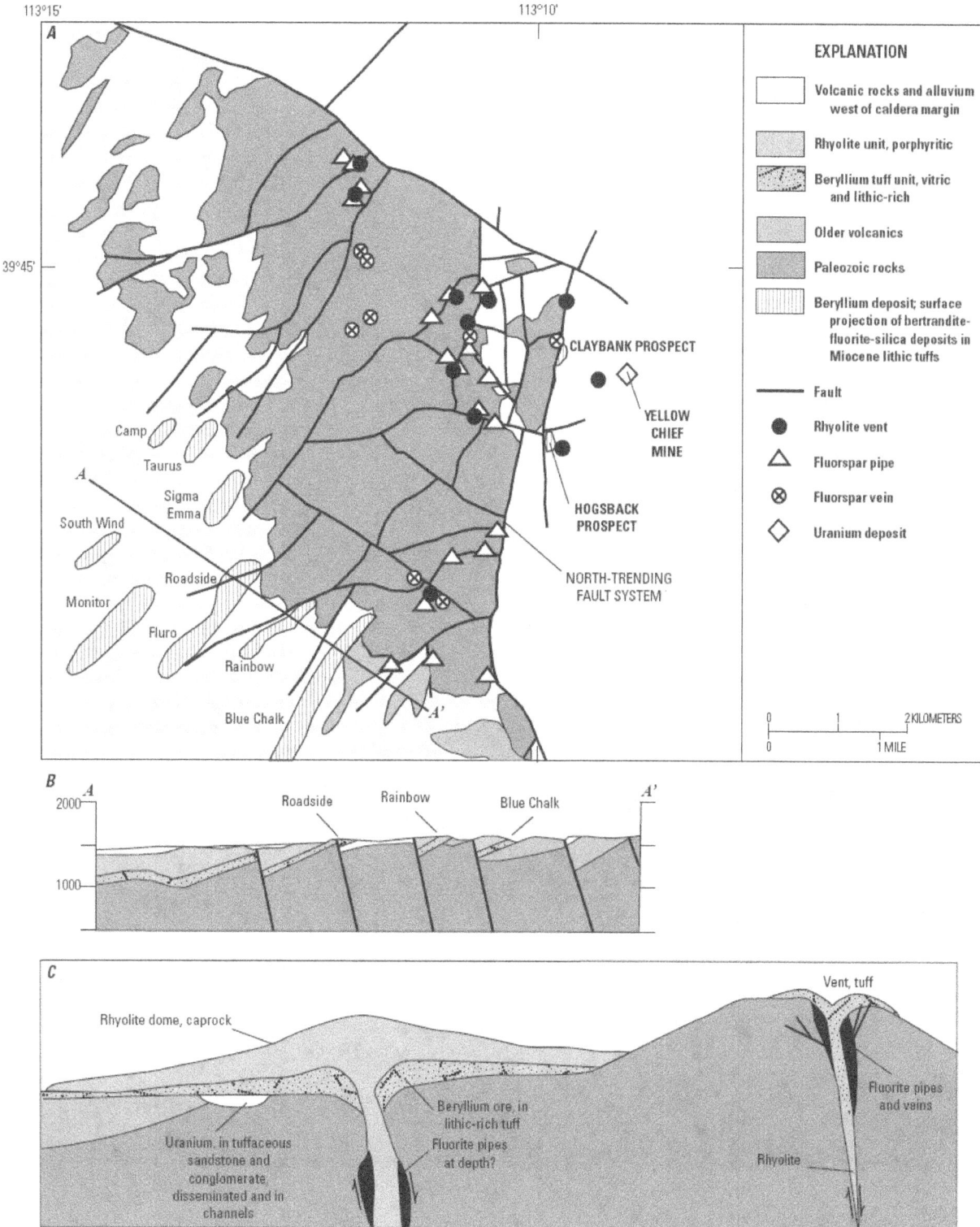

Figure 5. A geologic map of Spor Mountain area, Utah, showing (*A*) locations and distribution of beryllium (Be) deposits and fluorite pipes, Paleozoic carbonate rocks, the inferred boundary of the Thomas caldera, and volcanic rocks, mostly alluvium-covered, west of faults that mark the caldera margin (fig. 4); (*B*) cross section (location shown in fig. 5*A*) displaying the relation of the Be deposits to faults and the rhyolitic and tuffaceous host rocks; and (*C*) generalized cross section of the volcanic centers and their relation to Be, fluorite, and uranium deposits. Modified from Lindsey (2001).

Figure 6.   (*A*) Outcrop of beryllium tuff; photograph taken about 1969. (*B*) Roadside pit. Rhyolite caprock on right has been stripped to expose ore in the upper part of the beryllium tuff member of Spor Mountain Formation, about 1970. (*C*) Monitor pit. Porous, reactive beryllium tuff member initially composed of volcanic glass, zeolite, and abundant fragments of carbonate rock. Sample shows first stage of alteration of dolomite to calcite. The matrix is still glassy. (*D*) Beryllium tuff member after mineralization is composed of a matrix of clay and potassium feldspar; dolomite fragments are replaced by fluorite, clay, chalcedonic quartz, and manganese oxide. (*E*) Rainbow pit. Ore containing nodules (relict carbonate rock clasts) of clay outlined by purple fluorite. (*F*) Rainbow pit. Ore containing nodules of fluorite-dioctahedral smectite rimmed by chalcophanite. (From Lindsey, 1998).

Table 4. Chemical compositions of topaz rhyolite and melt components in the vicinity of Spor Mountain beryllium district (Christiansen and others, 1983, 1984; Lindsey and others, 1973; Lindsey, 1979a; Adams and others, 2009).

[na, not analyzed; ppm, parts per million; wt %, weight percent; Ma, million years ago]

	Topaz Mountain Rhyolite, Thomas Range, Utah (7–6 Ma)	Topaz rhyolite vitrophyre flow, Spor Mountain, Utah (21 Ma)	Unmineralized vitric tuff, Spor Mountain, Utah (21 Ma)	Spor Mountain Formation (21.73±0.19 Ma) and plug (21.56±0.07 Ma), melt inclusions in quartz (ppm)
Chemical composition (wt %)[2]				
SiO_2	75.9	73.9	69 (72.9)	
TiO_2	.09	.006	na (0.04)	
$Al2O_3$	12.9	13.1	10 (13.8)	
$Fe2O_3$	1.09	1.43	1.06 (1.12)	
MnO	.08	0.06	na (0.00)	
MgO	.09	.08	.74 (0.00)	
CaO	.74	1.27	1.83 (0.40)	
Na_2O	4.11	4.33	2.78 (4.60)	
K_2O	4.69	3.63	4.22 (5.10)	
LOI	-[1]	-[1]	5.8 (na)	
H_2O	-[1]	-[1]	4.6 (1.0)	
Cl	1,680	-	.22 (na)	
F	.64	1.06	.17 (1.2)	undetected to 1.4
Chemical composition (mg/kg)[2]				
Li	40	80	75 (137)	
Th	60	69	2.5 (61)	
U	15	38	45 (47)	
Be	6	52	7 (66)	undetected to 108 (average = 59)
Pb	na	na	34 (na)	
Ce	129	137	na (194)	

[1]Analysis recalculated H2O-free by Christiansen and others (1984).

[2]Data in parentheses is for SM-1, a unaltered vitrophyre chemically similar to vitrophyres of the beryllium tuff as reported by Webster and others (1989).

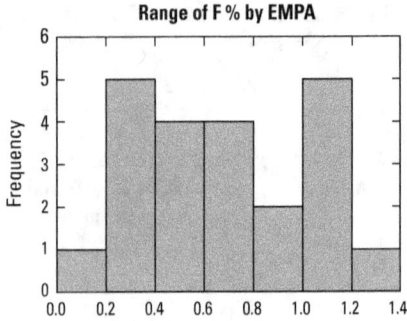

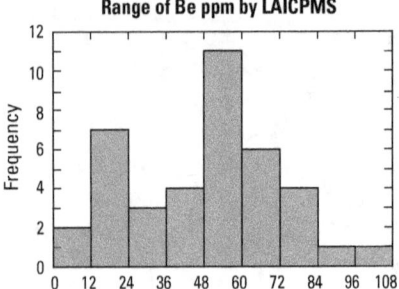

Figure 7. Histograms showing fluorine (F) and beryllium (Be) contents of melt inclusions in quartz phenocrysts from Spor Mountain beryllium tuff and a crosscutting 21.56-Ma intrusive plug. Fluorine by electron microprobe analysis (EMPA) and beryllium by laser ablation inductively–coupled plasma mass spectrometry (LAICPMS). Ppm, parts per million.

Duration of the Magmatic-Hydrothermal System and Mineralizing Processes

The timing and duration of Be ore formation spans the interval between the time of vent-related volcanism and the hydrothermal event(s) capable of remobilizing and concentrating Be. The hydrothermal event can be initiated as volcanism ceases or it can be superimposed on the volcanic tuff at a later time. For example, Be ores have the potential to form shortly after volcanism when deposition of lithic tuff is followed almost immediately by the development of hydrothermal cells capable of transporting Be. The Be is then leached from pumice, obsidian, or glass-filled vesicles. Alternatively, Be can be associated with the direct injection of magmatic lithophiles and precipitation of fluorite, opal, and bertrandite in replaced clasts, veinlets, and open space. Beryllium ore formation can continue for the duration of the magmatic-hydrothermal system, as long as metals, heat, and fluids are available. The concentrating process for Be ore can also occur long after the magmatism has ceased, resulting from leaching and redeposition of Be derived from volcanic glass by heated meteoric fluids.

Duration of Spor Mountain System

Ludwig and others (1980) demonstrated that the duration of the hydrothermal (magmatic-to-meteoric) system that included formation of the Be-mineralized nodules at Spor Mountain was long-lived, although the Be-mineralizing event(s) may have been episodic. They used uranium-lead isotopes of uraniferous opals from Spor Mountain to determine both the suitability of such material for geochronologic purposes and to estimate the potential timing of uranium-, beryllium-, and fluorine-bearing minerals by proxy. They showed that uraniferous opals can approximate a closed system for uranium and uranium daughters making possible the dating of opals as young as ≈1 Ma. By analyzing layers of opal intergrown with Be-bearing fluorite in nodules of the beryllium tuff member of Spor Mountain, they showed that a hydrothermal system or systems was potentially active for a period of almost 12 million years. In a single nodule, cores of opal and fluorite have an age of ≈20.8 ± 1.0 Ma, essentially coeval with volcanism. Ages of successive opaline layers decrease, clustering at ≈16 Ma and at ≈8.2 Ma. The outer opaline layers are the approximate age of the youngest volcanic rocks present in the region, the 7–6 Ma Topaz Mountain Rhyolite. These ages suggest episodic periods of opal (±fluorite-beryllium) deposition, which overlap the duration of topaz-rich volcanism but do not exclude continuous opal formation from a long-lived hydrothermal system punctuated by influxes of magmatic, lithophile-rich fluids. The relative importance of magmatic-hydrothermal fluids as a direct source of beryllium and fluorine, versus heated circulating meteoric fluids in remobilizing beryllium and fluorine along with silica from existing glasses, remains uncertain (see further discussion in Depositional Process section below).

Relations to Structures

Basin and Range fault development influenced eruption of the rhyolite lavas, deposition of pyroclastic surge deposits, and movement of hydrothermal fluids in the development of volcanogenic Be deposits at Spor Mountain district and at Apache Warm Springs, suggesting the importance of large-scale regional structures in the development of site-specific structural aspects of volcanogenic Be deposits. At Spor Mountain, displacements of Spor Mountain Formation and, locally, the younger Topaz Mountain Rhyolite, demonstrate repeated Basin and Range faulting, although some faults may have existed prior to eruption of rhyolites. Rhyolite plugs and domes that mark volcanic vents for Spor Mountain Formation, as well as Topaz Mountain Rhyolite, are located along faults and at fault intersections (fig. 5). A major north-trending fault system related to the Thomas caldera margin (figs. 4 and 5) is thought to have provided a regional control on mineralization (Lindsey, 1975). A set of southwest-trending faults leading off the north-trending fault system controlled the orientation of tuff-filled paleovalleys. Fluorspar-cemented breccia pipes that cut the Paleozoic carbonate rocks on Spor Mountain are also fault-controlled. At the Claybank beryllium prospect and the Bell Hill fluorite mine, breccia and wallrock in a reactivated margin fault are mineralized (Lindsey, 1998). The distribution of the mineralized zones suggests that the breccia pipe systems containing uraniferous fluorite and occurring along faults and fault intersections acted as conduits to channel mineralizing fluids through Paleozoic carbonate rocks (Staatz and Carr, 1964).

The Apache Warm Springs deposit, a part of the New Mexico-Arizona beryllium belt, is located on the northeastern edge of the Mogollon-Datil volcanic field in the Sierra Cuchillo Range. The original host lithologies were volcaniclastic rocks and rhyolite ash-flow tuffs (rhyolite of Alum Spring). The major structures in the region are related to Basin and Range faulting, and the mineralization is also localized in an area of intense faulting between two major graben structures that possibly make up part of a rhyolite dome structure.

Relations to Igneous Rocks

The Be tuffs are genetically related to volcanic and hypabyssal biotite-bearing topaz rhyolites and ongonites (Kovalenko and Kovalenko, 1976; Burt and others, 1982; Christiansen and others, 1984). The regional character of the associated igneous suites is bimodal and can consist of a broad compositional array from peraluminous to peralkaline igneous rocks, although the immediate host volcanic rocks are typically weakly peraluminous-metaluminous in composition and have enrichments in Be, F, Li, Nb, REE, Th, and U (Kovalenko and Kovalenko, 1976; Burt and others, 1982). Major provinces of topaz-bearing rhyolite and ongonites occur in the Western United States and the area of western Transbaikal, in Russia and Mongolia. The general characteristics and nature of topaz rhyolites of the Western United States have been described in detail by Burt and others (1982) and Christiansen and others (1983, 1984, 1986). The fluorine-rich magmas that produced the topaz-bearing rhyolite lavas are enriched in Be, Cs, Li, Rb, REE, Sn, Ta, Th, and U (table 3) and have been interpreted as being derived from varying degrees of protracted or extended differentiation (Christiansen and others, 1984). They are widely distributed across much of the Western United States and northern and central Mexico (Lipman and others, 1978; Turley and Nash, 1980; Burt and others, 1982; Christiansen and others, 1986).

Relations to Sedimentary Rocks

A critical factor in the formation of volcanogenic epithermal Be deposits is the presence of dolostone or limestone sequences that are the source of the reactive lithic clasts in the host tuff. At Spor Mountain, most of the Be resource occurs as replacement of angular to subrounded, variably altered carbonate fragments, primarily of light-gray dolomite, that range in size from a few millimeters to more than one meter in diameter. Breccia-filled volcanic pipes that cut the sedimentary rock sequence on the eastern side of Spor Mountain (for example, Staatz and Griffitts, 1961) provided avenues for pheatomagmatic eruptions that led to the formation of volcaniclastic surge deposits, which are high-velocity, relatively low-density, ground-hugging turbulent fluid flows capable of transporting lithics and ash (Burt and others, 1982). Locally, the tuffaceous deposits contain as much as 65-percent limestone, dolostone, and other lithics as pebbles, cobbles, and blocks, in addition to blocks of vitric tuff (Griffitts and Rader, 1963) in a matrix of pale-green to buff-colored volcanic ash (Shawe, 1968). Carbonate lithics are also reportedly common in pyroclastic rocks at the Holly Claims mine, Wah Wah Mountains, Utah (Burt and Sheridan, 1981), but are lacking in many other topaz rhyolites in Utah and throughout the Western United States (Burt and others, 1982). For example, at Apache Warm Springs, N. Mex., fault blocks to the south of the deposit indicate the area is underlain by Permian marine sedimentary rocks that include massive limestone. However, carbonate lithics are not characteristic of the host rhyolite of Alum Spring, and the Be minerals occur with clays in small quartz veins and stringers and disseminations in rhyolite and ash-flow tuff.

Relations to Metamorphic Rocks

Metamorphic rocks are not genetically associated with volcanogenic Be deposits.

Physical Description of Deposit

Deposit Dimensions

At Spor Mountain, the economic Be deposits consist of large, lens-shaped and tabular, stratabound bodies (Shawe, 1968) that are controlled by primary volcaniclastic layering and the original distribution of carbonate blocks and detritus within the vitric tuffaceous unit (Lindsey, 1977). The largest bodies of ore extend for as much as 4 km along strike over a down-dip distance of greater than 300 m and have thicknesses that may locally exceed 15 m. The tuff unit (fig. 6A) is as thick as 100 m, but it is also absent locally. Within the tuff unit, Be-rich layers range in thickness from less than 0.5 m to more than 6 m. The length of these layers along strike and down dip varies but can extend for more than 60 m. Weakly mineralized rock separates some of the mineralized layers and, locally, ore zones cut across bedding. The lateral extent of mineralization in the district is unknown because many new discoveries may be present on extensions of geologic structures and mineralized units that are concealed by overlying Pleistocene sediments. The surface expression of the Apache Warm Springs deposit, which is approximately 10 × 40 m, is comparable in size to one of the smaller individual deposits at Spor Mountain. The resource is estimated to contain ≈39,000 metric tons and may continue beyond the known extent (McLemore,

2010a). Thus, economic volcanogenic Be districts are likely to be made up of many small mineralized lenses that, as a whole, may cover 25 square kilometers or more but individually may cover only 100s of square meters.

Structural Setting(s) and Controls

A combination of stratigraphic and structural permeability provided pathways for mineralizing fluids to invade the Be-bearing tuffs and react with the carbonate lithic component that was the main chemical trap for these deposits. At Spor Mountain, fluorite-cemented breccia pipes that cut the Paleozoic carbonate rocks (fig. 5) are fault-controlled, and the breccia pipes served as conduits for hydrothermal fluids, although they themselves lack appreciable Be mineralization. As mineralizing fluids spread laterally from faults through permeable zones in the glassy tuff, they altered and replaced large areas of tuff, while leaving some adjacent formations relatively unaltered. Carbonate-rich lithics were the principal trap for beryllium- and fluorine-bearing minerals. Where hydrothermal solutions encountered zones of abundant carbonate clasts, fragments, or blocks in the tuffaceous surge deposits, they precipitated chalcedony, opaline quartz, additional fluorite, and Be-bearing minerals. At Apache Warm Springs, permeability in the tuff appears to have been controlled by fine stringers and veinlets; the absence of abundant carbonate clasts may have precluded the localization of Be in tuffaceous lithic-rich zones.

Geophysical Characteristics

Geophysical methods used in exploration for a specific deposit type rely primarily on the contrast of physical properties between juxtaposed formations and measure differences in magnetic susceptibility, electrical resistivity, radioactivity, and density between the host and ore bodies. Magnetic, gravity, and seismic data are useful in identifying large-scale geotectonic settings and igneous suites that are associated with volcanogenic Be deposits. For example, pronounced aeromagnetic (positive) and gravity (negative) anomalies outline the mineral belt that extends from Deep Creek Mountains, west of Spor Mountain, to the East Tintic Mountains in the east and include the volcanogenic Be deposits at Spor Mountain. This belt also contains occurrences of copper, other base metals, and gold in addition to scattered occurrences and deposits of fluorite and uranium (Park, 2006). The anomalies reflect, in part, the igneous stocks and thick accumulations of volcanic rocks that make up the calderas in the region. Aeromagnetic contours also delineate the configuration of doming within calderas in the region; for example, the Thomas caldera contains a central magnetic high that is thought to signify an intrusion of resurgent magma in the core. Aeromagnetic data for the Thomas caldera margin also reportedly show magnetic highs of ≈2,100 gammas at the west edge of the Thomas caldera, and the beryllium, fluorite, and uranium mines are located on the southwest flank of the magnetic high (Shawe, 1972). The causal relation between the deposits and the magnetic high is unknown, but the correlation is proposed to indicate favorable areas (Shawe, 1972). Magnetic anomalies near the Apache Warm Springs beryllium deposit have been used to suggest that the beryllium deposit continues south of the known extent in Red Paint Canyon (McLemore, 2010a).

The distribution and content of key minerals including magnetite, pyrite and other sulfides, calcite, dolomite, feldspar, and mica and clay minerals map differences in magnetic susceptibility, radioactivity, and density that potentially could be used to locate ore, although no examples are available for volcanogenic Be deposits. For example, hydrothermal alteration of magnetite in mineralized tuff may produce magnetic lows compared to surrounding volcanic rocks; the lows could target a Be deposit within unaltered (magnetite-bearing) tuff. Also, abundant and naturally occurring radioactive elements (potassium, uranium, and thorium) are part of the geochemical zoning signature that targets volcanogenic Be deposits. Elemental ratio maps prepared from gamma ray spectrometry survey data may be useful in delineating high-grade deposits by comparing thorium/potassium and uranium/potassium for mineralized and unaltered tuff. Remote sensing techniques such as advanced spaceborne thermal emission and reflection (ASTER) and airborne visible infrared imaging spectrometer (AVIRIS) may be useful in mapping hydrothermal alteration minerals that have distinctive spectral features and characterize Be deposits (Rowan and Mars, 2003). The use of shortwave infrared reflectance (SWIR) spectroscopy may allow for detailed mapping of alteration mineralogy. For example, AVIRIS SWIR data may be used to discriminate calcite from dolomite and identify hydroxyl-bearing clays, and as a result, identify zones in tuff potentially more favorable for Be ore.

Hypogene Ore and Gangue Characteristics

The Be ores that are the exemplar for this model have been described in detail by Staatz and Griffitts (1961), Griffitts and Rader (1963), Shawe (1968), Lindsey and others (1973), and Lindsey (1975, 1977, 2001). The following descriptions are based primarily on those reports, with comparisons to other occurrences. In this context, ore zones are generally defined as having >1,000 ppm Be in either the tuff matrix or in nodular materials that are both clay-rich and commonly feldspathic.

Mineralogy and Mineral Assemblages

The principal Be-bearing ore mineral associated with deposits of this model is bertrandite ($Be_4Si_2O_7(OH)_2$). The presence of bertrandite as the sole ore mineral is consistent with precipitation from hydrothermal fluids in a volcanogenic environment (Barton, 1986; Barton and Young, 2002 and references therein), whereas the presence of most other Be phases (beryl, euclase, helvite, phenakite, and bertrandite) is indicative of formation at higher temperatures (or pressures) not typical of epithermal environments (Barton, 1986). At temperatures above 400°C, beryl ($Be_3Al_2(SiO_3)_6$) is the stable Be-phase. It is completely replaced by euclase ($BeAlSiO_4(OH)$) over the range 300°C–400°C at moderate pressures. Phenakite (Be_2SiO_4) is stable at temperatures greater than 250°C and hydrates to bertrandite in the 300°C–200°C range. Bertrandite is stable at temperatures below 250°C and, thus, indicative of epithermal mineralization in near-surface settings.

Bertrandite is the sole Be mineral phase in volcanogenic Be deposits, although due to its fine-grain size and low abundance (<<5 percent by weight), it is difficult to identify by standard methods. At Apache Warm Springs, bertrandite is found with clay in small quartz veins and stringers, along fractures, and disseminated in the rhyolite lava and rhyolite ash-flow tuff. Primary minerals in the original host rock are replaced by mixtures of kaolinite, illite, quartz, hematite, and locally illite-smectite, pyrite, anatase, alunite, pyrophyllite(?) and bertrandite. At the Honey Comb Hills occurrence, beryllium (as much as 0.73 percent) is also associated with submicroscopic fluorite, montmorillonite, and kaolinite in stringers and veinlets; the Be may be present as submicroscopic bertrandite or sorbed onto mineral and or glass surfaces (McAnulty and Levinson, 1964). At Spor Mountain, beryllium-bearing mineral assemblages occur in both stringers and disseminations in tuff matrix and in nodules (figs. 6D, 6E, and

6F). The highest grade volcanogenic Be deposits consist of abundant nodules in mineralized tuff.

The Spor Mountain Formation tuff contains pore fillings, veinlets, and nodules of opal, manganese oxide minerals, fluorite (fig. 6E), clays (Be-bearing), and yellow secondary uranium minerals, including weeksite ($K_2(UO_2)_2(Si_2O_5)_3 4H_2O$) and beta-uranophane ($Ca(UO_2)_2(SiO_3OH)_2 5H_2O$). The clays are primarily dioctahedral smectites (fig. 6F), although Be-bearing smectite of the beidellite-saponite series is widespread in layers of mineralized tuff surrounding nodules. Ore nodules (figs. 8A, 8B, and 8C) consist of widely varying proportions of fine-grained calcite, silica minerals, fluorite, bertrandite (generally less than 2 percent by volume), clay, and manganese oxides. The distribution of Be in the assemblages is not restricted to nodules, and if it is elevated in the tuff matrix, then it is elevated in all layers in nodules, although bertrandite only occurs admixed with the fluorite layer.

Nodules can range from a few millimeters to 30 cm in diameter. They are typically sub-spherical in shape. Some replaced nodules and layers display complex alteration patterns (fig. 8A), but the simplest units consist of a fairly regular pattern of concentric and alternating zones, from core to rim, of calcite, chalcedony, opal, and outer fluorite + bertrandite (fig. 8B). In general, the nodules can be grouped into calcite-silica-fluorite-oxide types (fig. 8C) and fluorite-clay-manganese-oxide types (fig. 8A) (Lindsey, 1973).

Calcite and chalcedonic zones tend to be fairly monomineralic (80–90 percent). The gray-brown calcite present in cores of nodules formed by removal of magnesium from the

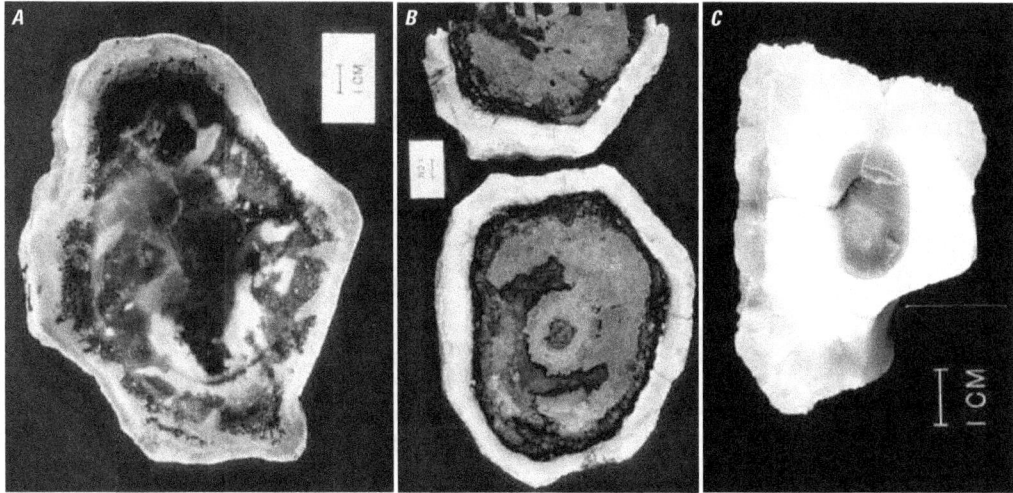

Figure 8. (A) Nodule from Roadside pit with an interior of quartz, opal, and fluorite and an outer zone of opal and fluorite that contains as much as 1-percent beryllium as bertrandite. (B) Nodule from Roadside pit with an interior of gray-brown calcite, an intermediate zone of black chalcedonic quartz, and an outer zone of white opal with minor fluorite. Beryllium is concentrated only in the outer opal-fluorite zone. (C) Fluorite-opal nodule from Monitor prospect yielded uranium/lead ages of ≈20.8 Ma (fluorite-opal core), ≈13 Ma (white opal middle zone), and ≈8 Ma (translucent opal rim). The ≈21-Ma age is indistinguishable from the age of the host beryllium tuff (Ludwig and others,1980). Photographs from Lindsey (1998).

original dolomite clasts (fig. 9A). Remnant textures include relict bedding, invertebrate fossil fragments, siliceous shells and detritus, and carbonate rock textures. Electron microprobe elemental maps (fig. 9B) demonstrate that magnesium is completely stripped from the carbonate, leaving mainly calcium and silicon. Silica minerals include quartz, which is typically cryptocrystalline and chalcedonic, opaline silica, and minor smectitic clays.

Fluorite (≥50 percent) and opal are often finely intergrown in Be-rich nodules. Fluorite-opal nodules (fig. 8C) can consist of as much as 1–2 percent Be as bertrandite but generally average ≈100 ppm Be (Lindsey, 1973). Fluorite ranges from purple, possibly a function of uranium content, to colorless and is typically cryptocrystalline (<<10 micrometers μm) grain size) and intergrown with equally fine-grained manganese oxide and silica minerals (fig. 10). Late fluorite crystals in vugs can exceed 50 m in width and can be zoned from colorless to purple (fig. 11A); the equant crystal form is typical of hydrothermal fluorite (fig. 11B). Manganese oxide minerals, including pyrolusite, cryptomelane, chalcophanite, and todorokite, occur with late fluorite and microcrystalline quartz as rinds and fracture fillings in nodules (fig. 11A). Bertrandite is submicroscopic and finely disseminated, concentrated mainly in the opal-fluorite stage of mineral deposition and has only been conclusively identified in fluorite layers in nodules. No uranium minerals have been identified in nodules, although both uranium and thorium occur as anomalous trace elements in fluorite and opaline silica.

Paragenesis

Beryllium nodules of the Spor Mountain district display a paragenetic sequence (fig. 12) that follows a uniform pattern: dolomite → calcite → chalcedonic quartz-opal → fluorite + bertrandite (Lindsey, 1977). Individual nodules may show all or part of the paragenetic sequence and monomineralic nodules are not uncommon.

The first stage in development of mineralized nodules was the removal of magnesium from dolomite by a dedolomitization reaction (equation 1):

$$CaMg(CO_3)_2 + H_2O = CaCO_3 + Mg^{-2} + HCO_3^- + OH^- \quad (1)$$

Calcium-carbonate and siliceous detritus remained in the nodules after the reaction. The release of magnesium and increase in alkalinity led to deposition of trioctahedral lithium montmorillonite, producing anomalous lithium and magnesium in tuff surrounding the ore zones.

The next stage in the paragenesis involved the replacement of carbonate clasts with successive layers of cryptocrystalline quartz or opaline silica + fluorite and beryllium. The

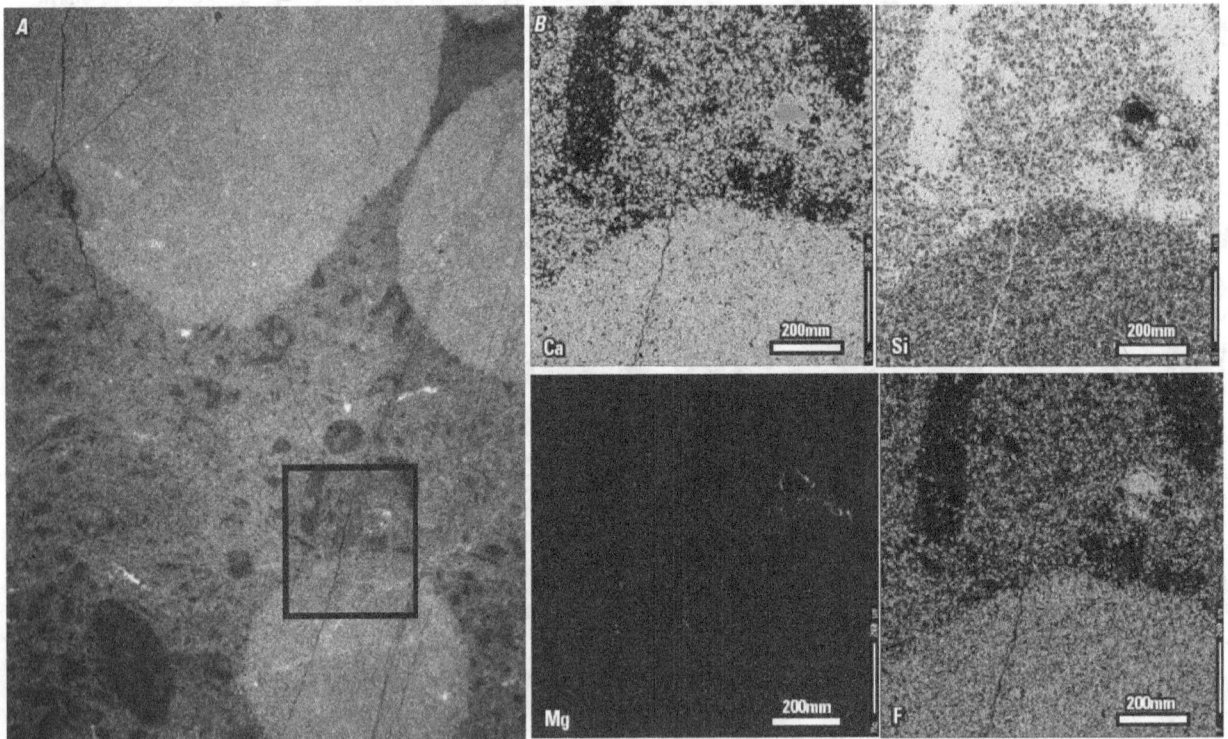

Figure 9.   (A) Siliceous shells and detritus in calcium-carbonate relic matrix being replaced by later fluorite mineralization. (B) Elemental maps by electron microprobe analysis for calcium (Ca), silicon (Si), magnesium (Mg), and fluorine (F) confirm that magnesium is completely stripped from the carbonate leaving a mix of mainly calcite and siliceous materials. The replacement front is primarily microcrystalline fluorite. A patch of coarser vuggy fluorite stands out in the calcium (red) map.

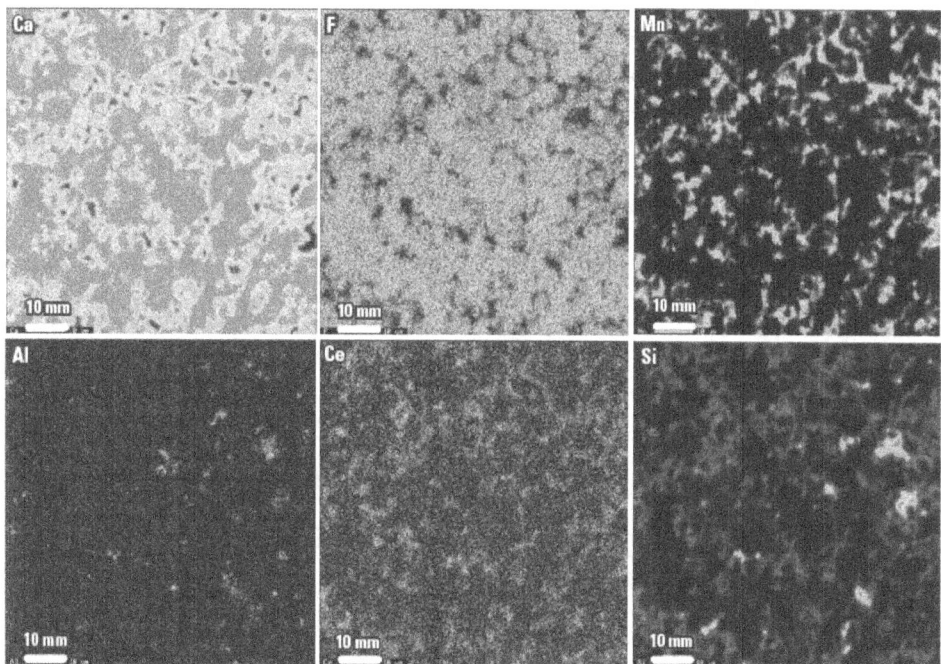

Figure 10. Textures typical of ore samples of volcanogenic beryllium deposits (example from Spor Mountain district). Electron microprobe elemental maps of calcium (Ca), fluorine (F), manganese (Mn), aluminum (Al), cerium (Ce), and silicon (Si), show typically massive fine-grained (<10 micrometers) fluorite admixed with cerium-bearing manganese oxide and minor clay (aluminum and silicon overlaps).

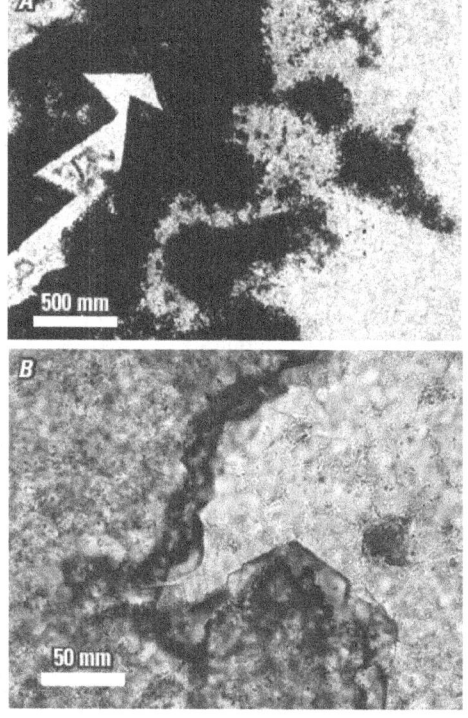

Figure 11. (*A*) Late fluorite and chalcedony in vug rimmed by manganese oxide minerals. (*B*) Purple fluorite and late quartz in vug.

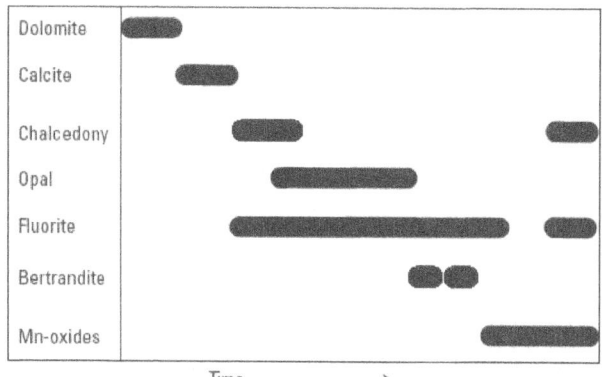

Figure 12. Generalized paragenetic sequence for beryllium-ore nodules of the Spor Mountain district shows the correlation of fluorite and bertrandite, a characteristic of volcanogenic beryllium deposits. Compiled from Staatz and Griffitts, 1961; Griffitts and Rader, 1963; Shawe, 1968; Lindsey and others, 1973; Lindsey, 1975, 1977, 2001; and this study. Mn, Manganese.

intimate association of finely crystalline intergrowths of fluorite and bertrandite supports co-precipitation. A reaction front showing the dissolution of calcite and precipitation of ore-stage minerals (fig. 9A) indicates infiltration of fluorine-bearing fluid and the wholesale replacement of calcite + siliceous detritus by cryptocrystalline fluorite, opal, and bertrandite.

At Spor Mountain, the combination of cryptocrystalline textures and botryoidal or colloform replacement structures is suggestive of silica supersaturation accompanied by rapid precipitation of opal and fluorite. Opal forms as colloidal particles of amorphous silica when a hydrothermal fluid becomes supersaturated with respect to quartz under rapidly changing conditions at temperatures below 200°C (Rimstidt, 1997). In contrast, the kinetics of fluorite precipitation are such that colloidal textures for fluorite are not usually indicative of supersaturation (Rimstidt, 1997). Deposition of fluorite-dominated ores from hydrothermal fluids can be accomplished by a number of mechanisms including temperature or pressure changes, fluid mixing, or as a result of wallrock interactions (Richardson and Holland, 1979). The most likely depositional mechanisms for fluorite associated with epithermal Be deposits of this type are wallrock reactions that cause a change in pH and cooling of the circulating hydrothermal fluid by conduction (Wood, 1992). Fluorite formed by reaction of calcite in nodules with a slightly acidic fluorine-bearing hydrothermal fluid (equation 2) results in the generation of bicarbonate, an increase in pH of the hydrothermal fluid, and the release of Be^{++} from the breakdown of fluoride complexes.

$$\text{Calcite} + 2\ F^- + H^+ = \text{Fluorite} + HCO_3^- \qquad (2)$$

The formation of bertrandite (equation 3) is a function of the general activity of silicic acid in a hydrothermal fluid, and the precipitation of bertrandite tends to lower the pH of the residual fluid.

$$4\ Be^{++} + 2\ SiO_2(aq) + 5\ H_2O = \text{Bertrandite} + 8\ H^+ \qquad (3)$$

An overall reaction (equation 4) describing the replacement process shown in figure 9 may be of the form

$$4\ \text{Calcite} + 4\ BeF_2(aq) + 2\ SiO_2 + H_2O = 4\ \text{Fluorite} + 4\ CO_2(g) + \text{Bertrandite} \qquad (4)$$

where BeF_2(aq) stands in for the various fluoride complexes of Be and SiO_2 for the polymorphs of quartz (Wood, 1992).

Zoning Patterns

The Be ores at Spor Mountain are generally restricted to layered, stratified tuff breccias that occur just beneath the rhyolite lava flow member of the Spor Mountain Formation (fig. 6B). Mineralized tuff can contain more than one discrete Be-rich layer (Staatz and Griffitts, 1961). At most places in the district, Be ore zones are concentrated in the upper part of the

beryllium tuff member (Lindsey, 1977). The Roadside orebody (fig. 6) is a type locality where dolomite clasts in the upper part of the member are mainly replaced by concentrically zoned layers of calcite, opaline silica, and fine-grained fluorite with submicroscopic inclusions of bertrandite. Below and outside of the ore zones, the original dolomite clasts are altered to calcite and contain anomalous amounts of lithium, probably in associated smectite alteration minerals. In the lowest part of the beryllium tuff, dolomite clasts are unmineralized and generally unaltered. Other clasts of quartzite, limestone, and volcanic rock are relatively unaltered outside the upper part of the beryllium tuff member. At other orebodies in the district, Be-rich layers occur in the middle and (or) lowermost sections of the member. For example, at the Blue Chalk deposit at Spor Mountain, Be is found in the lowermost section near the base of the tuff. Small mineralized zones also occur in the lower part of the overlying topaz-bearing rhyolite of Spor Mountain Formation.

Hydrothermal Alteration

Volcanogenic Be deposits are associated with distinctive alteration assemblages on regional to local scales. Regionally, Be-bearing tuffs may be extensively altered with a mineralogical signature consisting of diagenetic clays and K-feldspar. In the vicinity of high-grade Be deposits, the tuff matrix may be subjected to intense potassium feldspathization associated with sericite and smectite; an assemblage that halos highly mineralized lenses and likely resulted from intense hydrothermal alteration. Distinct geochemical signatures recognized regionally that may result from hydrothermal alteration include Be, Cs, F, Ga, Li, Nb, and Y and in the immediate vicinity of Be ore lenses, CaO, F, Li, and MgO may be elevated.

The bulk mineralogical and major and trace element geochemical characteristics of hydrothermally altered and mineralized beryllium tuff at Spor Mountain are summarized in table 5, along with data for unmineralized vitric tuff (Lindsey and others, 1973). Beryllium, CaO, F, Li, and MgO are elevated and montmorillonite, cristobalite + opal, and K-feldspar are abundant in mineralized tuff compared to relatively unaltered and unmineralized vitric tuff. At Spor Mountain, Lindsey and others (1973) attribute all features of the K-feldspar + montmorillonite alteration to the interaction of circulating cooling hydrothermal fluids with a concomitant rise in pH and decline in fluorine concentrations. However, the deposit alteration patterns described for Spor Mountain reflect an overprinting of hydrothermal and diagenetic processes that are indistinguishable on the basis of currently available data. The significance of the spatial distribution of the feldspathic alteration, in particular, is open to question because elemental (Be, Cs, F, Li, Ga, Nb, and Y) dispersion patterns surrounding orebodies (described below under Zoning Patterns) reportedly appear unrelated to K-feldspar alteration (D. Burt, Arizona State University, written commun., 2011). Distinguishing low temperature hydrothermal alteration caused by circulating mixed magmatic-meteoric fluids from diagenesis caused by burial and percolating groundwater is often difficult because many aspects of eodiagenesis and mesodiagenesis are poorly understood, particularly with respect to mineralogical modifications attributable to residence time, fluid chemistry, burial depths, and mass transfer. Thus, some of the alteration assemblages described here apply to tuffs in general and may not fingerprint Be-mineralized tuff.

Argillic and Feldspathic Alteration

The degree of pervasive alteration of tuff seen at Spor Mountain is extremely significant in comparison to known subeconomic occurrences and unmineralized tuff (Lindsey, 1975, 1977). Unmineralized tuff contains as much as 80-percent pumice; as much as about 14-percent primary quartz, sanidine, plagioclase, and biotite; and trace magnetite, ilmenite, topaz, sphene, and zircon in a glassy (vitric) or zeolitic tuff matrix. Zeolitic tuff may show alteration patterns in a mineralogical sequence of glass + vesicular pumice → smectite (montmorillonite clay) and matrix → clinoptilolite. A distinctive geochemical attribute of the altered and mineralized volcanic units is the presence of lithium-bearing trioctahedral smectites, which closely follow and enclose Be-rich ore zones.

The intensely mineralized Be zones within the volcanic units are accompanied by alteration of the volcanic constituents (Lindsey and others, 1973). Mineralized tuff contains variable amounts of altered pumice, volcanic clasts, and dolomite pebbles and as much as 20-percent primary quartz, sanidine, plagioclase, and oxidized biotite.

Table 5. Mineralogy and chemical composition of unmineralized (vitric) and mineralized tuff, Spor Mountain and Thomas Range, Utah. From Lindsey and others (1973).

[All values are medians. The maximum values (in parentheses) are also given where the median falls below the detection limit or where large variation is present; mg/kg, milligrams per kilogram; -, not detected]

Alteration assemblage	Vitric (unmineralized)	Argillic (mineralized)	Feldspathic (mineralized)
Number of samples	10	8	8
Mineral composition (weight percent)			
Montmorillonite[1]	-	66	9
Mica[2]	-	1	<1
Clinoptilolite	14	<1 (40)	-
Quartz	4	5	9
Cristobalite[3]	3	5	25
Potassium feldspar[4]	11	18	52
Calcite	1	1 (23)	-
Dolomite	-	1 (5)	-
Fluorite	<3	3	4
Halite	<1	<1	1
Glass[5]	66	<1	-
Chemical composition (weight percent)			
SiO_2	69	64	64
Al_2O_3	10	11	11
Fe_2O_3[6]	1.06	1.28	1.30
MgO	0.74	1.98	1.42
CaO	1.83	2.46 (14.00)	2.90
Na_2O	2.78	2.40	2.39
K_2O	4.22	2.69	5.10
LOI[7]	5.8	8.6	5.5
CO_2	0.5	0.45 (9.91)	0.06
H_2O[8]	4.6	7.36	5.53
C[1]	0.22	0.45 (1.15)	0.31 (1.75)
F	0.17	1.22	1.82

Table 5. Mineralogy and chemical composition of unmineralized (vitric) and mineralized tuff, Spor Mountain and Thomas Range, Utah. From Lindsey and others (1973).—Continued

[All values are medians. The maximum values (in parentheses) are also given where the median falls below the detection limit or where large variation is present; mg/kg, milligrams per kilogram; -, not detected]

Alteration assemblage	Vitric (unmineralized)	Argillic (mineralized)	Feldspathic (mineralized)
Number of samples	10	8	8
Chemical composition (mg/kg)			
Li	75	230	315
Tl	2.5	3.5 (19.9)	6.1 (54.0)
U	45	65	85
Be	7	105	14 (250)
Cr	9	5	<5
Cu	3	3	3 (43)
Fe	8,700	9,100	10,500
Mn	700	510 (3,400)	805 (8,000)
Ni	<7	<7 (7)	<7
Pb	34	37	42
V	14	17	11
Zn	<300	<300 (340)	150 (1,600)

[1]Dioctahedral montmorillonite clay; quantity determined by difference

[2]Biotite plus secondary sericite

[3]Includes some opal

[4]Sanidine plus secondary potassium feldspar

[5]Quantity determined by difference

[6]Total Fe and Fe_2O_3

[7]Loss on ignition (LOI) at 900 C for 1 hour

[8]LOI minus CO_2

The alteration products include abundant montmorillonite (both dioctahedral and trioctahedral smectites), calcite, opal, manganese oxide minerals, feldspar, and minor kaolinite (described below). The alteration forms a distinctive envelope of argillized and feldspathized tuff surrounding the high-grade deposits (Staatz 1963; Shawe, 1968). The volcanic units are incompletely argillized, and vitric and zeolitic components remain in mineralized tuff. Argillic tuff can contain as much as 80 percent montmorillonite, as much as 5-percent fluorite, and no additional feldspar, as well as fragments of fresh glassy pumice, volcanic rock, and carbonate rock. Feldspathized tuff represents a more advanced and complete degree of alteration. It is identified by the presence of abundant feldspar, in excess of unmineralized tuff, and as overgrowths of clear potassium feldspar on volcaniclastic fragments and on sanidine. It also includes α-cristobalite, which may have formed by recrystallization of amorphous silica by hydrothermal fluids, and as much as 40-percent montmorillonite and 8-percent fluorite.

Kaolinitization

Kaolinitic alteration that is present near volcanogenic Be deposits may be secondary and unrelated to mineralization processes. Kaolinitization of volcaniclastic rocks, including dissolution of lithics, feldspar, and mica, is common, and, in general, the resulting spatial distributions of eogenetic kaolinite are typically related to groundwater-flow patterns at the time of deposition or to paleotopography (for example, Morad and others, 2000). For example, kaolinitic alteration that cuts bedding and roughly parallels paleotopography at Spor Mountain is probably unrelated to Be ore. The widespread zeolite and kaolinite likely formed by diagenetic alteration caused by burial of the deposits by overlying Pleistocene sediments of Lake Bonneville.

Supergene Ore Characteristics and Processes

Supergene processes are not thought to be a factor in enhancing Be ore grade. Further work is needed to fully evaluate the importance of the observed kaolinite and zeolite assemblages (Lindsey, 1975) and identify any elemental redistribution caused by supergene processes related to, for example, burial conditions and the possible incursion of modified lake fluids. In the Pleistocene, the alkaline closed-basin Lake Bonneville covered much of northwestern Utah, and at Spor Mountain, gravels, sands, silts, and indurated marls that compose sedimentary beds of the Lake Bonneville Group overlay the Be deposits and the youngest volcanic rock sequences. Supergene processes acting on the tuffs are implicated in remobilization of U, F, and Mn during zeolitization and, thus, may have overprinted some geochemical zoning patterns related to Be mineralization. Furthermore, zeolitization is thought to have caused relative depletions in the tuff in Na, K, F, Rb, U, Mn, and Pb.

Geochemical Characteristics

Trace Elements and Element Associations

Processes of hydrothermal alteration imparted a distinct geochemical signature on the beryllium tuff. Anomalous amounts of uranium (100–200 ppm) and thorium (100–150 ppm) are broadly associated with Be ore, although the anomalies may be offset from the orebodies by 10s of meters (Lindsey, 1981), possibly due to later remobilization by groundwater. For example, at the Roadside orebody, tuff immediately underlying (within 5–10 m) Be ore contains 100–200 ppm U, whereas the ore zone averages 50–100 ppm U. Ten to 20 m below the ore zone, uranium contents drop sharply to <25 ppm. The higher values of uranium are associated with the abundance of a lithium-bearing smectite. In contrast to uranium, the major thorium anomaly (100–150 ppm) at the Roadside orebody is within the Be ore. Thorium levels outside the Be ore zone are in the range of 50–100 ppm (Lindsey, 1981). The ratio of thorium/uranium in the Be-bearing ore zone is generally <2, whereas it rises to >4 at about 30 m beneath the ore zone.

Zoning Patterns

An association of elements, including F, Cs, Li, Be, Ga, Nb, and Y, compose primary dispersion halos that act as vectors to both Be ore and fluorite deposits at Spor Mountain (Lindsey, 1975). Other trace and minor constituents locally enriched in the halos include manganese, zinc, and tin. Most of the elements thought to be related to Be mineralization form primary dispersion halos that extend as far as 3.2 km from Spor Mountain into unaltered tuff. Thus, the geochemical halos form a target on the order of 156 km² that encloses the Spor Mountain district (covering ≈52 km²). Lindsey (1975) documented sharp declines in concentrations of cesium (from 100 to 2 ppm), lithium (from 300 to 15 ppm), and beryllium (from >200 to <5 ppm) over a distance of 8 km from Spor Mountain. The element dispersion patterns are distinct and apparently unrelated to zeolitization and potassium feldspar diagenesis of the tuffs. Thus, distinctive trace element anomalies measured in unmineralized tuff can serve as vectors to

volcanogenic Be ore, and the extent of the halos provides an approximate measure for the assessment target.

Fluid-Inclusion Microthermometry

Fluid inclusion studies of volcanogenic Be deposits are uncommon because of the fine-grained, cryptocrystalline nature of the mineral phases. A study of atypical vuggy vein material from the Fluoro pit at Spor Mountain did yield limited homogenization temperature data for quartz and fluorite in the range of 143°C–163°C (Murphy, 1980). General estimates of temperatures of formation of volcanogenic Be deposits are between 100°C and 200°C, based on fluid data for Spor Mountain, low-temperature mineralogy (bertrandite versus phenakite), and fine-grain size (Murphy, 1980; Burt and Sheridan, 1981; this study).

Stable Isotope Geochemistry

In a preliminary study of hydrogen and oxygen isotope signatures of unaltered rhyolite, altered rhyolite, and Be tuff at Spor Mountain, Johnson and Ripley (1998) report evidence for the involvement of both magmatic and meteoric waters in alteration and ore deposition. Measured $\delta^{18}O$ values of unaltered porphyritic rhyolite range from 8.4 to 9.1 ‰ (parts per thousand), whereas $\delta^{18}O$ values for altered rhyolite are in the range 9.3–11.7 ‰. δD values of unaltered rhyolite (–120 to –135 ‰) are lower than values typically associated with igneous rock fully equilibrated with magmatic fluids, suggesting a model involving devolatilization and D-depletion in the residual melt. The $\delta^{18}O$ (9.7–11.8 ‰) and δD (–92 to –120 ‰) values of the Be tuff define a geochemical front that requires a model involving both magmatic fluids and meteoric waters, suggesting that heated convecting waters leached Be and other lithophile elements from topaz rhyolite to form deposits. A magmatic fluid component is consistent with the introduction of fluorine, an important criterion because fluorite is present along faults in carbonate rocks below the beryllium tuff member.

Radiogenic Isotope Geochemistry of Ore

Compositions of nonradiogenic lead and uranium measured on opal in nodules from the beryllium tuff member of Spor Mountain suggest that isotope data cannot be used to distinguish volcanic units that host volcanogenic Be deposits from unmineralized topaz rhyolite; the compositions show no distinctive attributes that might be used to fingerprint Be mineralization of this type. Uranium contents of opals at Spor Mountain range from 21.8 to 1,030 ppm and lead contents range from 1 to 129 ppm. Decay-corrected $^{206}Pb/^{204}Pb$ (17.97–20.17) and $^{207}Pb/^{204}Pb$ (15.62–15.74) and blank-corrected $^{208}Pb/^{204}Pb$ (38.30–39.65) values (Ludwig and others, 1980) are similar to those that might be expected from the volcanic rocks of the area as compiled by Zartman (1974).

Depositional Process

Although there is a paucity of empirical data available to model hydrothermal fluid compositions for volcanogenic Be deposits, some parameters can be constrained. Wood (1992) provided a geochemical model for Spor Mountain mineralization based on an analysis of available thermodynamic data for Be complexes and observed mineral assemblages. The hydrothermal fluid was unlikely to have had a pH of <3, because alteration minerals such as alunite are not present and potassium-feldspathic alteration reactions would tend to buffer the pH of the system at higher values. The predominance of K-feldspar over minerals such as gibbsite and kaolinite also suggests a limited range of K^+/H^+ values; muscovite-sericite is present in only minor amounts. The activity of silicic acid in the fluid may have been relatively low (that is, quartz-saturated) in the ascending fluid. However, during deposition, it was likely buffered at a range of values controlled by the presence of the abundant silica minerals (cristobalite), smectite, and volcanic glass. Beryllium may have been leached from volcanic glass in the tuff by hydrothermal fluids during devitrification and hydrothermal alteration. Melt inclusions in quartz phenocrysts from a topaz rhyolite plug and Be tuff each contain ≈59 ppm Be, whereas devitrified glass of the Be tuff contains about 7 ppm (table 4). It is unlikely that the mineralizing fluids contained more Be than the potential local sources, which include devitrified glass (>7 ppm) and melts (≈59 ppm), because the ascending magmatic fluids did not leave an appreciable Be signature in fluorite-filled vent structures. Thus, Be values in the range of 0.5 to 5 ppm are reasonable for a mineralizing fluid. Wood (1992) proposed a value of 1 ppm Be in the fluid and established that the most feasible means of transporting Be in hydrothermal fluids below 250°C is in complexes with fluoride. The activity of free fluoride at mineralization sites at Spor Mountain was likely buffered by the production of fluorite, but may have been higher in the volcanic rock sequence if controlled by reactions involving fluorotopaz (Wood, 1992).

A simple model illustrating a reaction path, such as the one suggested by the replacement front shown in figure 9, can be constructed based on the general parameters listed in table 6. The values calculated by Wood (1992) provide for a fluid capable of both transporting sufficient components to the deposition site as fluoride complexes and of precipitating varying amounts of fluorite, quartz, and bertrandite. The results (fig. 13) suggest that simple cooling of the fluid would precipitate minor amounts of fluorite, with F^- supplied by the breakdown of aluminum-fluoride species, but not bertrandite because the solubility of Be-fluoride species would increase slightly with cooling as a result of declining pH. In contrast, an isothermal (≈150°C) or cooling fluid (≈150°C to 100°C) encountering carbonate clasts would result in precipitation of the alteration assemblages and fluorite and bertrandite in a ratio of 100:1, which is comparable to that seen in nodules. Clinoptilolite in the tuff would convert to amorphous silica, muscovite, or K-feldspar, depending on changes in activity of K^+ and H^+ as mineralization proceeded. This model does not provide a unique solution because most of the intensive parameters, including pH and temperature, are not well-constrained and the fluid composition can only be approximated from the described assemblages.

Table 6. A model hydrothermal fluid composition for Spor Mountain.

[Modified based on thermodynamic estimates and other data from Wood (1992)[1] and Murphy (1980)[2]. Mg/kg, milligrams per kilogram; ppb, parts per billion, ppm; parts per million; --, no unit]

Parameter	Unit	Fluid characteristic
Temperature	°C	200–100[1]; (160–140[2])
pH	--	4–6 (no alunite, K-feldspar alteration); near-neutral[1]
SiO_2(aq)	--	Activity fixed by cristobalite
Ca, Al, K	--	Estimated by alteration assemblage of K-feldspar, Ca-clinoptilolite, beidellite-Ca (montmorillonite), rare sericite (muscovite)
HCO_3	mg/kg	100
Cl	mg/kg	1,000
F	--	>0.01 molal[1] or fixed by fluorite[1]
Mn	mg/kg	1
Be	mg/kg	1[1]; (500 ppb–5 ppm)
Saturated phases	--	Bertrandite, quartz, fluorite, pyrolusite

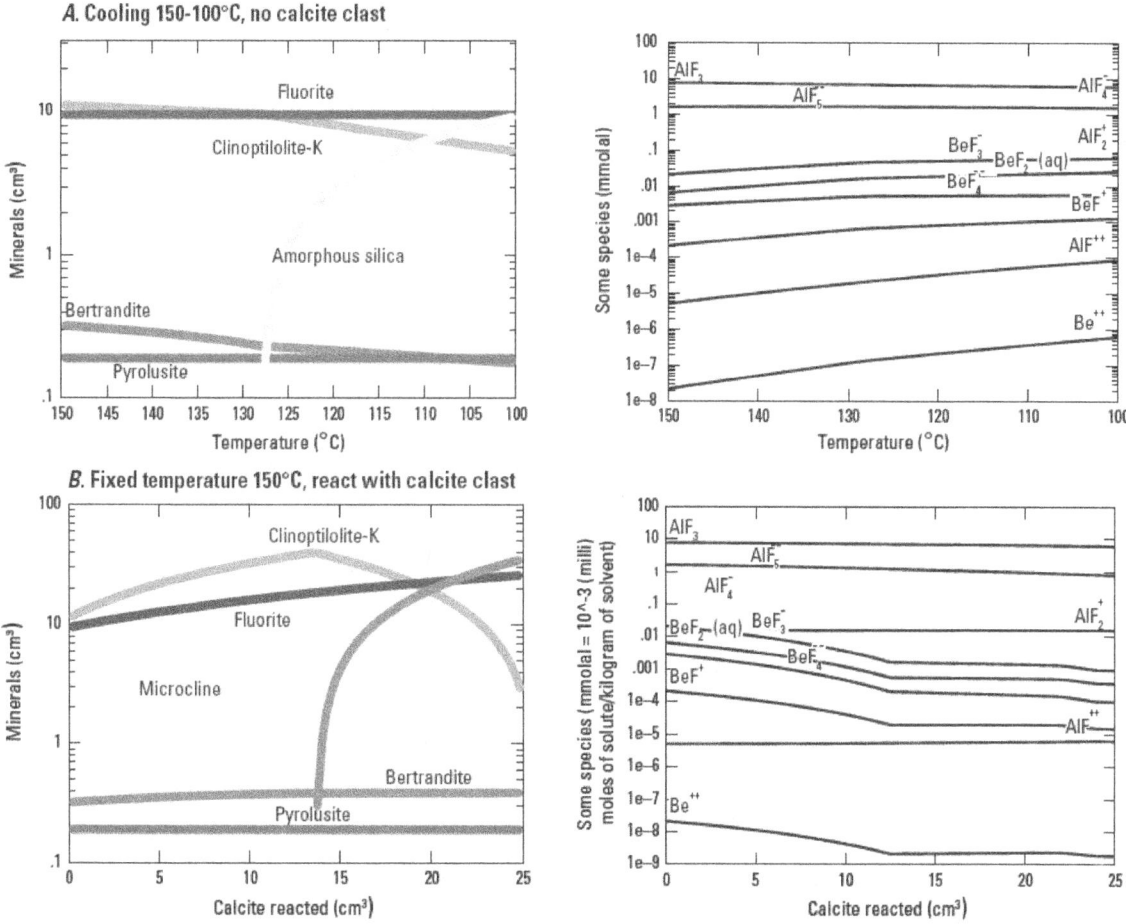

Figure 13.   Simplified reaction paths models for the formation of fluorite replacement front in beryllium ore nodules based on the geochemical model for the Spor Mountain district of Wood (1992). (*A*) Simple cooling of a hydrothermal fluid (by conduction) from 150°C to 100°C. A small amount of fluorite is predicted to precipitate; however, bertrandite is less stable with declining temperature. (*B*) Interaction of a 150°C hydrothermal fluid with carbonate clast. The reduction of beryllium fluoride complexes in solution leads to precipitation of fluorite and bertrandite as the replacement proceeds. Diagrams were calculated using Geochemist's Workbench and a standard database modified with beryllium data from Wood (1992) and the WATEQ4F database (a chemical speciation database for natural waters) from Ball and Nordstrom (1991). Mmolal = 10^{-3} moles of solute/kilogram of solvent.

Petrology of Associated Igneous Rocks

Volcanic and hypabyssal high-silica rhyolite and granite porphyry constitute the most well recognized igneous suites associated with volcanogenic Be deposits (Christiansen and others, 1984). The magmatic compositions of igneous rocks associated with nonpegmatitic hydrothermal Be deposits are invariably reported as felsic, although the general compositions can cover the range from strongly peraluminous and metaluminous to peralkaline. Igneous systems hosting volcanogenic Be deposits, such as those found at Spor Mountain, are metaluminous to weakly peraluminous in bulk composition. Elemental enrichments associated with these high-silica topaz-bearing rocks include variable amounts of F, Li, Mo,

Nb, Sn, and Ta; they may contain phenakite, bertrandite, and helvite-group minerals.

Christiansen and others (1984) described the geochemical evolution of topaz rhyolites and associated pyroclastic deposits exposed in the Thomas Range and at Spor Mountain in west-central Utah. The rhyolites are part of a regional late Cenozoic bimodal sequence of basalt and rhyolite volcanism that typified the Great Basin beginning about 22 Ma (for example, Best and others, 1980). In general, rhyolites of the bimodal sequence are enriched in fluorine, to as much as 1.5 percent by weight Be, Li, U, Rb, Mo, Sn, and REE. The rhyolites occur as part of a distinct assemblage of topaz-bearing lavas that are distributed across much of the Western United States and northern Mexico and whose general characteristics are described in detail by Christiansen and others (1983, 1986). The best examples are those from the southern end of the Thomas Range near Topaz Mountain, the type locality for Topaz Mountain Rhyolite.

Both the Spor Mountain and Thomas Range sequences were deposited episodically, which began with the emplacement of a series of pyroclastic breccia, flow, phreatomagmatic base surge, and air-fall deposits and ended with eruption of rhyolite lavas (Bikun, 1980; Burt and Sheridan, 1981). Both volcanic rock sequences contain topaz, which is indicative of fluorine enrichment (>0.2 percent) and have an aluminous nature (Lindsey and others, 1973). The younger lavas and tuffaceous units of the Topaz Mountain Rhyolite were emplaced from at least 12 eruptive centers (Lindsey, 1979b). The underlying topaz rhyolite member of Spor Mountain Formation has an $^{40}Ar/^{39}Ar$ age of 21.56±0.07 Ma (Adams and others, 2009) and was likely emplaced from a much smaller number of vents active at that time (Lindsey, 1982). This rhyolite and the subjacent beryllium tuff member occurred in isolated and tilted fault blocks on the southwestern side of Spor Mountain and as remnants of domes and lava flows on the eastern side of the mountain. The rhyolite at Spor Mountain contains higher concentrations of fluorine and lithophile elements than the Topaz Mountain Rhyolite. Christiansen and others (1984) documented the extreme enrichment in incompatible trace elements in the lavas. They proposed that concentrations of fluorine in the evolving Spor Mountain rhyolite (table 3) drove residual melts to less silicic compositions with higher sodium and aluminum and promoted extended differentiation yielding rhyolites extremely enriched in Be, Cs, Rb, Th, and U at moderate SiO_2 concentrations (74 percent). Christiansen and others (1984) consider that the rhyolite at Spor Mountain may have evolved from a magma generally similar to that of the Topaz Mountain Rhyolite, but its differentiation was more protracted. They propose that extended fractional crystallization, possibly aided by liquid fractionation, could have led to extreme concentrations of Be, Cs, Li, Rb, and U. Further, they postulate that the magmatic concentrations of these elements set the stage for the development of the Be-mineralized tuff member, which underlies the rhyolite.

There are a number of potential mechanisms for inducing a system to generate explosive volcanism; however, magma mixing is the favored mechanism for the Spor Mountain Formation (Christiansen and others, 1983). The injection of hot mafic magma into colder felsic magma can trigger vigorous convection leading to catastrophic magmatic degassing and explosive venting in subvolcanic plutons (for example, Sparks and others, 1977) and extensive brecciation of and mineral deposition in surrounding rocks (Hattori and Keith, 2001). For example, the influx of primitive melt into the lower levels of an upper crustal felsic magma system and subsequent mixing to produce a hybrid rhyodacitic melt may trigger volcanic activity. Consequent decompression of the magma system would result in the release of lithophile-bearing vapor. Large

explosive eruptions can have both magmatic and phreatomagmatic components. The presence of cross-bedded volcanic base surge deposits preserved beneath a lava flow of topaz rhyolite provided evidence for the involvement of magma and water in the explosive volcanism at Spor Mountain (Burt and Sheridan, 1981). In this case, the eruptions are presumed to be the result of interaction between magma and water in an aquifer. Important criteria in the recognition of the phreatomagmatic surge deposits at Spor Mountain are the presence of coarse angular clasts, a lack of sorting, laminar bedding and cross bedding, bomb sags, and position of the deposits beneath a rhyolite dome complex that is adjacent to a volcanic vent.

Petrology of Associated Sedimentary Rocks

At Spor Mountain, the thick sequence of Paleozoic marine carbonate and clastic rocks, which provided the carbonate lithics in the tuff, formed on a continental shelf margin (Staatz and Griffitts, 1961). The generally conformable sedimentary rock sequence ranges in age from Early Ordovician to Devonian, and the following description is summarized from Shawe (1968) and Lindsey and others (1975). Limestones of the Garden City Formation, shales and quartzites of the Swan Peak Formation, and the Fish Haven Dolomite compose the Ordovician section. This section is overlain by the Ordovician or Silurian Floride Member of Ely Springs Dolomite and the Silurian Bell Hill, Harrisite, Lost Sheep, and Thursday Members of Laketown Dolomite. The Devonian units include the Sevy Dolomite and carbonates of the Engelmann Formation. The Ordovician section contains gray thin-bedded limestone and tan-to-pink, weathered, medium-bedded limestone, thin beds of green shale, intraformational conglomerate and interbedded red quartzite, thick-bedded white vitreous quartzite, and massive black-mottled dolomite. The Silurian section is chiefly composed of gray dolomite, locally calcareous, which ranges from thin-bedded and fine-grained to massive, dark-gray and coarse-textured sand. Some of the Silurian dolostones contain bands of gray and (or) pink chert, are blue-gray and mottled, and fossiliferous (*Halysites*). The Devonian section consists mainly of fine-grained thin to medium-bedded gray-laminated dolomite and local light-gray to black limestone.

Below an elevation of ≈1,600 m, the Tertiary volcanic rocks and the underlying and older sedimentary rock sequences at Spor Mountain are partly covered by gravels, sands, silts, and indurated marls of the Pleistocene to Holocene Lake Bonneville Group. The Lake Bonneville deposits drape up against a number of small and low foothills of sedimentary and volcanic rocks that formed adjacent to Spor Mountain and may conceal additional Be deposits in tuff at depth.

Petrology of Associated Metamorphic Rocks

Metamorphic rocks are not genetically associated with volcanogenic Be deposits.

Theory of Deposit Formation

Formation of volcanogenic Be deposits is due to the coincidence of multiple factors that include an appropriate Be-bearing source rock, thermal fluid drivers, a depositional site, and a delivery system for concentrating the ore minerals. Setting the framework for formation of the uniquely economic Be mineralization was a sequence of events that are described based on Spor Mountain. This sequence of events links critical aspects of an evolving system leading to the formation of economic deposits of volcanogenic Be.

Sequence of Events

1. Both the tuff and flows of the Miocene Spor Mountain Formation contain quenched enclaves of mafic magma (Christiansen and Venchiarutti, 1990). Injection of the hot, volatile-rich, mafic magma into highly evolved rhyolite magma chambers triggered eruptions.

2. The eruption at 273±19 Ma (Adams and others, 2009) of the beryllium tuff member of Spor Mountain Formation resulted in pyroclastic breccia, base surge, flow, and air-fall deposits (Christiansen and others, 1984; Burt and others, 2008).

3. Eruption of porphyritic topaz rhyolite member of Spor Mountain Formation occurred from at least three vents in plugs, domes, and flows (Lindsey 1982) and included formation of vapor-phase minerals such as topaz (Christiansen and others, 1984). Relict sanidine from an altered plug-dome has been dated at 256±07 Ma (Adams and others, 2009).

4. Diagenesis of beryllium tuff member (and perhaps the base of rhyolite flows) included formation of widespread zeolite (clinoptilolite) ± potassium feldspar (Lindsey, 1975).

5. Hydrothermal activity followed with deposition of (a) fluorite, with little or no Be-bearing minerals in pipes, veins, and faults in Paleozoic carbonate and Oligocene volcanic rocks below the beryllium tuff member at Spor Mountain; (b) disseminated deposits of fluorite that are Be-bearing in rhyodacite, rhyolite, and tuff; and (c) concentrations of bertrandite, amorphous silica (opal), fluorite, clay minerals (hectorite), and potassium feldspar in the beryllium tuff, particularly at the former sites of lithic fragments of dolomite (Lindsey, 1977).

6. The oldest $^{207}Pb/^{235}U$ apparent age of opal at approximately 28±1 Ma, from the opal-fluorite core of a nodule (Ludwig and others, 1980), is essentially coeval with the age of the rhyolite host rocks. Outer layers of uraniferous opals yielded dates that fall into two groups at 16–13 Ma and 9–8 Ma. Other uraniferous opals found in calcite- and fluorite-bearing fractures in volcanic rocks as young as 6 Ma yielded ages of 5–3 Ma. This range in ages may reflect episodic hydrothermal activity and (or) groundwater movement (Ludwig and others, 1980).

7. Undated supergene weathering resulted in remobilization of uranium, decoupled from thorium, and deposition of secondary oxidized uranium beneath Be-rich zones and in fluvial sandstones below the Spor Mountain Formation, including potentially economic accumulations such as at the Yellow Chief mine.

Genetic Model

A genetic model that illustrates the development of stages of mineralization for volcanogenic epithermal Be deposits constructed by Burt and Sheridan (1981) is shown in figure 14. The stages described below relate the sequence of events to the components and processes of mineralization:

Stage 1—Igneous source: High-silica, lithophile-rich magmas capable of producing volcanic and hypabyssal high-silica biotite-bearing topaz rhyolite and granite porphyry compose the source material. Barton and Young (2002) calculated that a small amount of a hypothetical Be-bearing magma (0.4 km³ at 3.6 ppm Be) would be required to make a world-class deposit such as Spor Mountain (see fig. 1). They compared that with the 100 km³ or more that is required for most metals in most other deposit types. However, the much higher median concentration of Be (59 ppm) in melt inclusions measured for Spor Mountain (Adams and others, 2009) suggests that an even smaller minimum volume of magma (0.135 km³) or tuff (0.272 km³) is required to provide sufficient Be (fig. 15). If Be was derived solely from tuff, then a block 1 km wide × 5 km long × 54 m thick is required to account for the Be ore in the district. These calculations for minimum volumes of rock necessary to form such a deposit assume extraction efficiencies of 100 percent. Lower extraction efficiencies would require substantially larger volumes of rock (fig. 16). The low average concentration of 7 ppm Be in the clinoptilite- and adularia-altered vitric tuff at Spor Mountain compared to melt inclusions (average ≈59 ppm) and unaltered vitrophyre (66 ppm) suggests an extraction efficiency on the order of 90 percent for the glassy matrix. Thus, a substantial amount of Be was potentially leached from the estimated 10 km³ of tuff erupted in the region (Lindsey, 1982).

Stage 2a—Driver: A mechanism is required that would result in explosive lithophile-rich rhyolite volcanism and vigorous convection leading to catastrophic magmatic degassing and explosive venting in subvolcanic plutonic systems, the

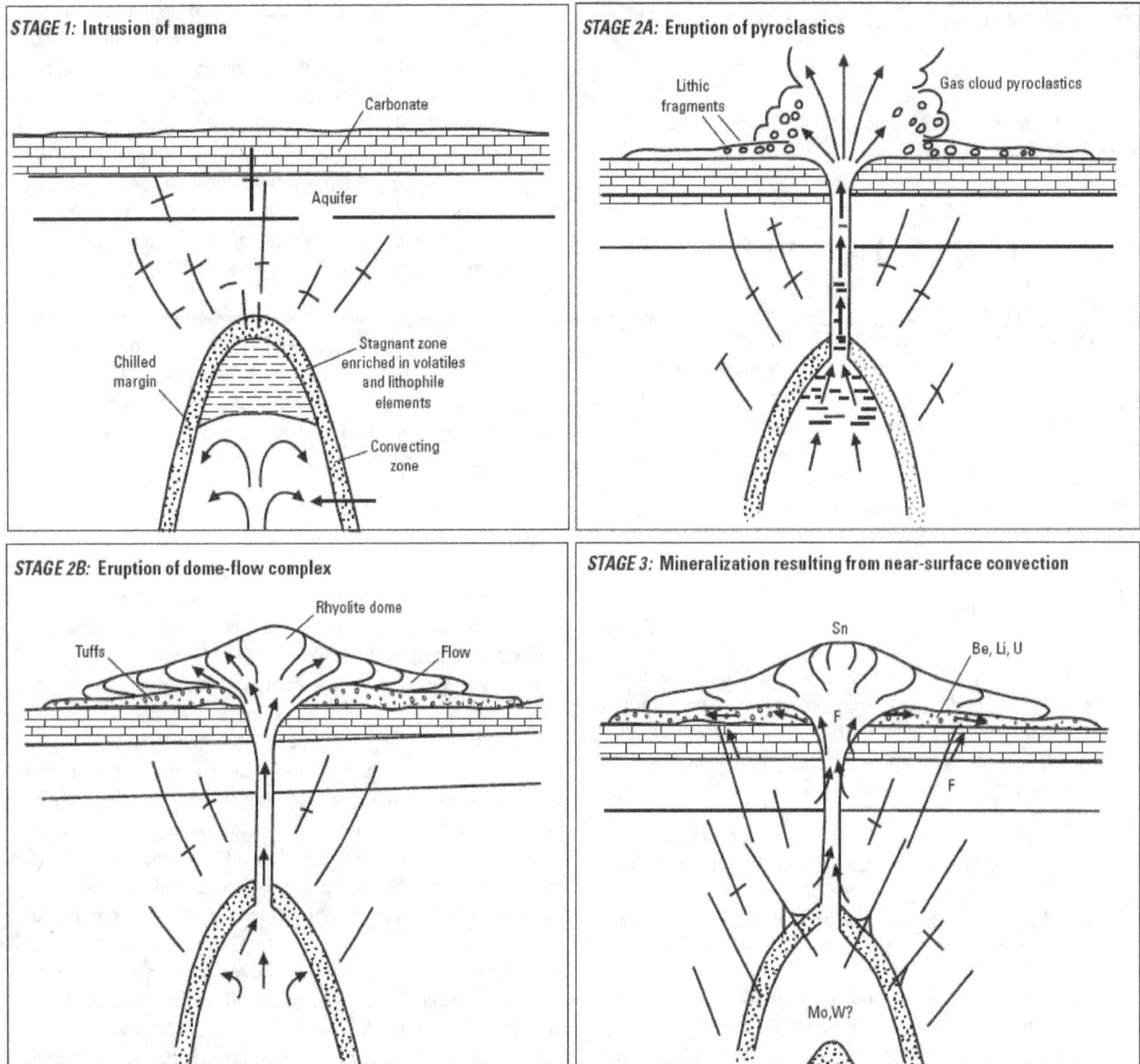

Figure 14. A general model for formation of volcanogenic deposits of uranium (U), beryllium (Be), and other lithophile elements as proposed by Burt and Sheridan (1981). Sn, tin; Li, lithium; F, fluorine; Mo, molybdenum; W, tungsten.

release of lithophile-bearing magmatic vapor phases from the felsic magma, and the potential for forming carbonate clast-rich volcanic surge deposits in tuff. Christiansen and others (1984) proposed that magma mixing in the chamber is an effective mechanism for generating the catastrophic degassing and venting. They consider that the fluorophile element (for example, Be, Cs, Li, U, and Rb) enrichments in the Spor Mountain rhyolite magma resulted from extended fractional crystallization aided by liquid fractionation. The Be-bearing glasses in the tuff contribute geochemical and mineralogical components to hydrothermal fluids.

Stage 2a—Site: Basin and Range fault development influenced eruption of the rhyolite lavas, deposition of pyroclastic surge deposits, and the movement of hydrothermal fluids in the Spor Mountain district. High-angle fault systems within the district provided regional controls on mineralization and pipes. Faults through the underlying carbonate rocks acted as conduits to channel mineralizing fluids to the Be-bearing tuff. Breccia-filled volcanic pipes that cut the underlying sedimentary rock sequence signal the explosive volcanism that generated carbonate lithic-rich phreatomagmatic base surge deposits. The pipes provided avenues for magmatic fluids to

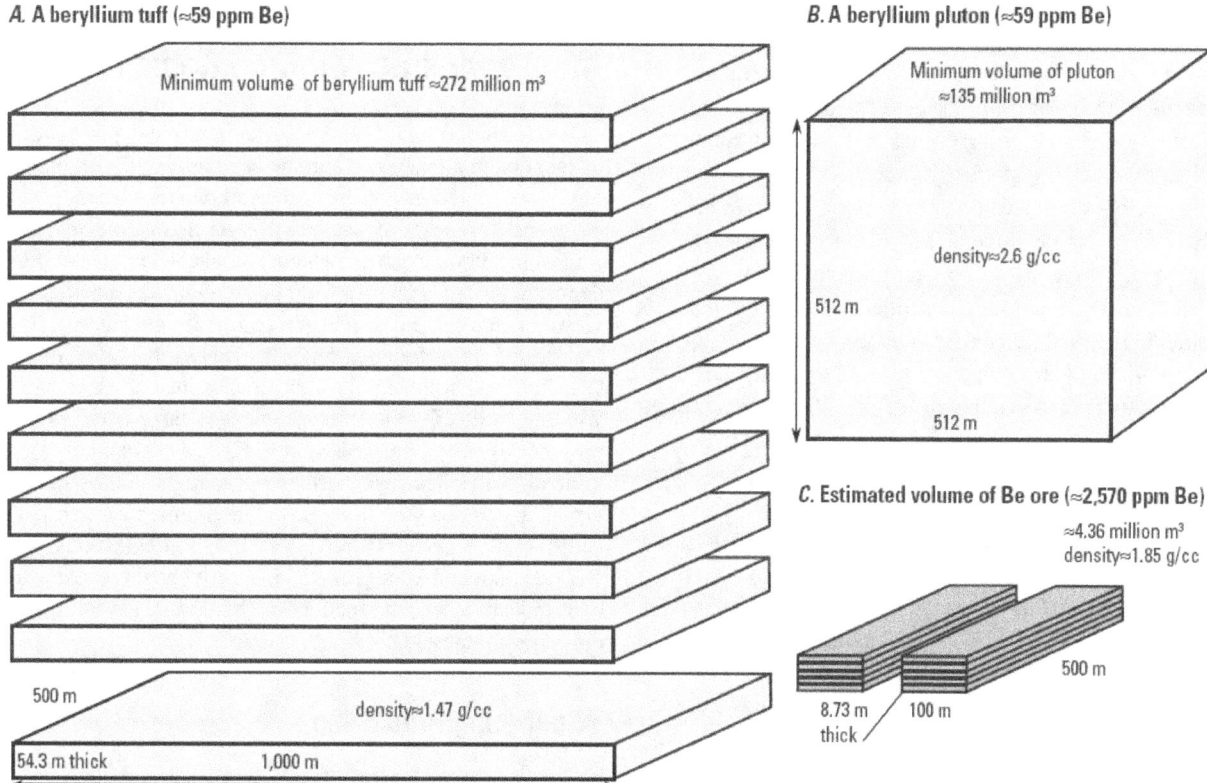

A. A beryllium tuff (≈59 ppm Be)

Minimum volume of beryllium tuff ≈272 million m³

500 m

density≈1.47 g/cc

54.3 m thick   1,000 m

B. A beryllium pluton (≈59 ppm Be)

Minimum volume of pluton ≈135 million m³

density≈2.6 g/cc

512 m

512 m

C. Estimated volume of Be ore (≈2,570 ppm Be)

≈4.36 million m³
density≈1.85 g/cc

500 m

8.73 m
thick   100 m

Figure 15. Minimum volumes of tuff or pluton required to form beryllium (Be) resource at Spor Mountain. (*A*). Volume of tuff (272 million m³, d (density) =1.47 gram/cubic centimeter (g/cc); corrected for presence of phenocrysts and carbonate in tuff; 59 parts per million (ppm) Be that must be completely leached of Be to form the ore corresponds to a block (shown as stack of 10 slabs) 54.3 m thick, 1 km wide, and 0.5 km long. This volume makes models that call upon mobilization of Be from altered tuff permissive. (*B*). Volume of pluton required to account for amount of Be in ore is smaller than amount of tuff because its density is higher (2.6 g/cc, 135 million m³). This corresponds to a cube about 0.5 km on a side, which is similar in size to cupolas that form important porphyry deposits. Thus, models that call upon release of volatiles from cooling plutons also are permissive. (*C*). Relative volume of Be ore (4.36 million m³, d=1.85 g/cc, 2,570 ppm Be) is shown in ten stacked bodies 500 m × 100 m × 8.75 m. These bodies are comparable in dimension to some of the larger individual ore lenses of Spor Mountain (for example, see fig. 3).

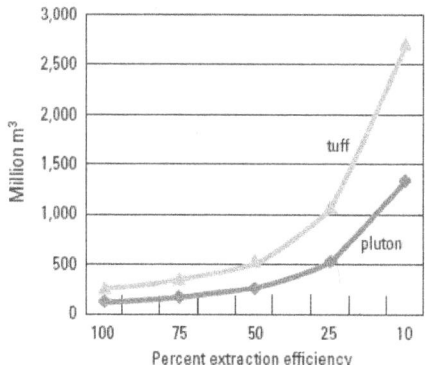

Figure 16. Plot showing extraction efficiency (percent) versus volume (million m³).

reach and interact with meteoric fluids and eventually generate the hydrothermal cells capable of leaching Be from volcanic glass in the tuff. At the depositional site, carbonate lithics and ignimbritic textures of the tuff supplied both porosity and permeability, and Be-bearing glasses in the tuff contributed geochemical and mineralogical components.

Stage 2b—Confined system: The position of the Be tuff between relatively impermeable Paleozoic rocks and a younger topaz rhyolite lava flow confined circulating hydrothermal fluids to the porous and permeable tuffaceous breccias and stratified vitric tuff. This set the stage for focused, potentially long-lived hydrothermal fluid flow through the tuff.

Stage 3—Delivery system: Leaching of large volumes of lithophile-rich volcanic source rock by a large-scale hydrothermal system can provide the beryllium, fluorine, and other lithophile elements that characterize the ores. At Spor Mountain, hydrothermal leaching of the Be tuff led to deposit formation; however, the role of shallow degassing of magma, with or without deep Be mineralization, cannot be excluded (Wood, 1992; Barton and Young, 2002). Mineralization processes involving both magmatic fluids (Staatz and Griffitts, 1961; Shawe, 1968; Lindsey and others, 1973) and heated meteoric fluids (Burt and Sheridan, 1981) have been proposed, but the relative roles of Be introduction by ascending magmatic fluids versus leaching of Be from volcanic glass by circulating shallow heated meteoric groundwater remain uncertain.

Stage 3—Trap: A vital factor in development of the depositional trap for the richest Be ore was the incorporation of dolomite as lithic fragments in volcanic surge deposits, which formed as a result of explosive phreatomagmatic eruptions (Burt and Sheridan 1981). The highly reactive dolomitic fragments encased in tuff were subsequently mineralized by interaction with fluorine- and beryllium-bearing hydrothermal fluids, and the replaced fragments now form beryllium-rich nodules.

Formation of the mineralized nodules has two distinct aspects. Initially dolomite fragments are converted to calcite by removal of magnesium, and, subsequently, calcite is replaced by successive layers of rhythmically banded chalcedonic quartz and opal and fine-grained bertrandite-bearing fluorite. Thus, the overall hydrothermal process involves a combination of dissociation, dissolution, and precipitation. The conversion of dolomite to calcite caused subsequent precipitation of magnesium smectites. Mineralization proceeded with dissolution of calcite and precipitation of varying forms of silica, fluorite, and bertrandite. The proposed mechanism for precipitation (Lindsey and others, 1973; Lindsey, 1977; Wood, 1992) is the declining fluorine activity as cooling hydrothermal fluids encountered carbonate in the tuff. Changes in pH and temperature of the fluid are factors in fluorite precipitation. Bertrandite precipitation is favored by loss of the fluoride ligand during precipitation of fluorite, as well as the associated changes in pH and activity of silica.

Geoenvironmental Features and Anthropogenic Mining Effects

The uniqueness of the Spor Mountain Be deposit and its location in a fairly arid climate have limited the amount of geoenvironmental information available for volcanogenic Be deposits. Despite the paucity of information, meaningful insights into the geoenvironmental characteristics of this deposit type can be gained from its geologic characteristics viewed in the context of relevant regulatory guidance. Key features of Spor Mountain-type Be deposits that relate directly to their geoenvironmental characteristics include association with high-silica rhyolites; replacement of carbonate rocks; presence of bertrandite ($Be_4Si_2O_7(OH)_2$) as the main ore mineral, with silica, calcite, fluorite, potassium feldspar, and clays; association with fluorine and uranium enrichments; and sulfide-poor character (Lindsey and others, 1973; Lindsey, 1977; Barton and Young, 2002). Collectively, these features contribute to a deposit type for which minimal environmental concerns are present.

Weathering Processes

From an environmental perspective, weathering processes associated with mine wastes from processing ore are dominated by the weathering of remnant bertrandite, fluorite, and uranium-bearing minerals from a mineralogically poorly defined source. Lindsey (1981) speculated that uranium at Spor Mountain is hosted by uraniferous fluorite or opal. Bertrandite, the primary ore mineral, presumably occurs in mine waste in minor amounts due to imperfect grinding of ore prior to ore processing.

The environmental geochemistry of Be deposits and their associated mine wastes has been the subject of few studies (Deubner and others, 2001; Stefaniak and others, 2008). More general information is also available on Be in the environment (Veselý and others, 2002; Taylor and others, 2003).

Most of the environmental concerns associated with Be deposits focus on airborne particles associated with ore and metallurgical processing (Deubner and others, 2001; Stefaniak and others, 2008). Nevertheless, the dissolution of bertrandite can be described by the reaction

$$Be_4Si_2O_7(OH)_2 + 8\ H^+ \rightarrow 4\ Be^{2+} + 2\ H_4SiO_4 + H_2O \qquad (5)$$

or the reaction

$$Be_4Si_2O_7(OH)_2 + 8\ H^+ \rightarrow 4\ Be^{2+} + 2\ SiO_2 + 5\ H_2O \qquad (6)$$

in the presence of quartz or amorphous silica (Wood, 1992). The solubility of Be is expected to be extremely low ($<1\ \mu g/L$), except under low pH (<3.5) conditions (fig. 17). Due to the lack of sulfide minerals to generate acid and the abundance of limestone at Spor Mountain, low pH conditions are unlikely

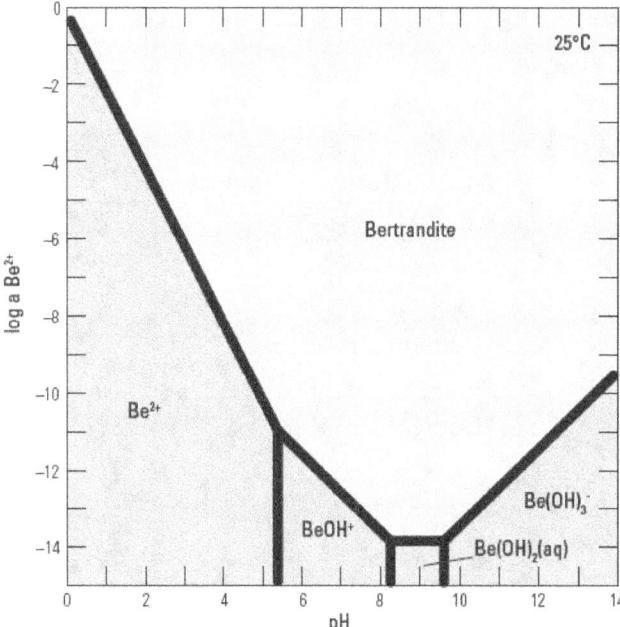

Figure 17. Diagram showing the solubility of bertrandite and the dominant speciation of dissolved beryllium (Be) as a function of log aBe^{2+} and pH at 25°C. The activity of silica was buffered by the presence of quartz in the calculations. Diagram was calculated using the Geochemist's Workbench using the data from Wood (1992) and WATEQ4F (a chemical speciation database for natural waters) from Ball and Nordstrom (1991).

associated with the deposit. However, the Be extraction process from bertrandite ores involves acid leaching at high temperature using sulfuric acid (Stonehouse, 1986). Thus, such ore-processing practices could potentially lead to Be discharge to surface water and groundwater in the vicinity of the ore-processing facility.

Pre-Mining Baseline Signatures in Soil, Sediment, and Water

Pre-mining baseline geochemical data surrounding the Spor Mountain deposits are essentially lacking. Bolke and Sumsion (1978) conducted a reconnaissance hydrologic study in the Fish Springs Flat area, covering an area of 27 × 56 km in Tooele, Juab, and Millard Counties, Utah, which includes the Spor Mountain mine. Precipitation averages 18 cm per year. Stream flow is ephemeral and mainly due to thunderstorms or snowmelt. The more widespread regional dataset indicates that groundwater in the Fish Springs Flat area is neutral to slightly alkaline (pH 7.2 to 8.0) and is characterized as being slightly saline to briny (specific conductance 2.89 to 34.70 millisiemens per centimeter). The only element of environmental concern included in the analyses presented by Bolke and Sumison (1978) was fluoride, which reached a

maximum concentration of 4.0 milligrams per liter (mg/L) in one sample located more than 30 km from the mine. Groundwater samples nearer the mine site had fluoride concentrations of 0.4 to 2.9 mg/L (table 7). For comparison, the maximum contaminant level for drinking water is 4 mg/L (table 8).

In the absence of site-specific data for volcanogenic Be deposits, Be concentrations in average crustal rocks and soils offer a useful reference in the absence of baseline data from unmined deposits. The average upper crustal abundance of Be is 3.1 milligrams per kilogram (mg/kg). Concentrations in soils range from 0.1 to 300 mg/kg with a global average of 6 mg/kg (Veselý and others, 2002). However, global values of Be in soils are thought to be high in comparison to soils in the United States, and soils and regolith of the arid western States of Utah and New Mexico have Be contents of generally less than 1.5 ppm (Shacklette and Boerngen, 1984).

Past and Future Mining Methods and Ore Treatment

Ores at Spor Mountain are mined by open-pit methods. The sheet-like ore zone ranges between 0.6 and 12 m in thickness (Hawkins, 2001). The ores undergo a series of crushing and chemical extraction steps to produce either a Be-carbonate ($BeCO_3$) or Be-hydroxide ($Be(OH)_2$) product (Stonehouse, 1986). The crushed ores are ground to less than 20 mesh. The resulting slurry is leached with sulfuric acid at elevated temperature resulting in an aqueous solution containing approximately 0.7 grams per liter (g/L) beryllium, 4 to 7 g/L aluminum, 3 to 5 g/L magnesium, and 1.5 g/L iron. Further processing strips the Be from this solution.

Volume of Mine Waste and Tailings

The ore at Spor Mountain averages 0.3-percent Be (0.72 weight percent BeO) with a total tonnage of approximately 7 Mt (Lindsey, 2001). Mining occurs with a stripping ratio (waste rock:ore) of 23:1 (Hawkins, 2001). Because of the low grade of the ore, essentially all of the mined and processed ore becomes waste.

Mine Waste Characteristics

Chemistry

Due to the low concentration of Be in the ore, the geochemistry of the mineralized tuff should be representative of most of the bulk geochemical characteristics of the waste material. The geochemical characteristics of the mineralized tuff at Spor Mountain have been summarized by Lindsey and others (1973). The data, summarized in table 5, come from both argillically and feldspathically altered mineralized tuffs, which contain some carbonate clasts. For the most part, the major-element data reflect the rhyolitic protolith (Si> Al> K>

Table 7. Geochemical characteristics (dissolved) of groundwater in the vicinity of the Spor Mountain deposit, Utah. From Bolke and Sumsion (1978).

[mS/cm, millisiemens per centimeter; mg/L, milligrams per liter; μg/L, micrograms per liter; --, no value]

Parameter	Unit	Mine site[1] (C-13-12)5cbd-1	Nearby[1,2] (C-12-12)10cbc-S1	(C-14-12)4cbc-1
Temperature	°C	16.5	22.0	23.0
pH	--	--	7.3	--
Specific conductance	mS/cm	2.89	8.40	4.05
SiO$_2$	mg/L	3.2	31	52
Ca	mg/L	130	690	110
Mg	mg/L	53	170	72
Na	mg/L	410	870	650
K	mg/L	5.1	18	23
HCO$_3$	mg/L	180	227	360
SO$_4$	mg/L	340	380	300
Cl	mg/L	610	2,500	980
F	mg/L	0.6	2.9	0.40
Fe	μg/L	150	120	20
Mn	μg/L	20	100	10
B	μg/L	320	490	1,100

[1]The groundwater temperatures are higher than expected for nonthermal groundwater in the area; the total range reported by Bolke and Sumsion (1978) for the area is from 16.5 C to 60.5 C and includes data for hot springs. The paucity of field measurements for the dataset precludes normalizing for temperature or effects.

[2]Nearby samples are located within 15 km of the mine site.

Table 8. Environmental guidelines relevant to Spor Mountain Be deposits.

[Criterion: LOEL, lowest observable effects level; TLV, threshold level value. Sources: CCME, Canadian Council of Ministers of the Environment; NIOSH, National Institute of Occupational Safety and Health; USEPA, United States Environmental Protection Agency; WHO, World Health Organization. Mg/L, micrograms per liter; mg/kg, milligrams per kilogram; mg/m^3, micrograms per cubic meter; --, no value]

Medium/criterion	Units	Beryllium	Fluorine	Uranium	Source
Human health					
Drinking water	mg/L	4	4,000	--	USEPA (2009)
	mg/L	50	1,500	15	WHO (2008)
	mg/L	--	1,500	20	CCME (2010)
Residential soil	mg/kg	160	--	230	USEPA (2009)
	mg/kg	--	--	23	CCME (2007)
Industrial soil	mg/kg	2,000	--	3,100	USEPA (2009)
	mg/kg	--	--	300	CCME (2007)
Air (TLV)	mg/m^3	2	2,500	200	NIOSH (2005)
Aquatic ecosystem health					
Surface water acute (LOEL)	mg/L	130	--	--	USEPA (1980)
Surface water chronic (LOEL)	mg/L	5.3	--	--	USEPA (1980)

Ca ≈ Na> Fe ≈ Mg). The trace-element data show notable enrichments in beryllium, fluorine, and uranium relative to unmineralized counterparts.

Mineralogy

The mineralogical characteristics of the mineralized tuff at Spor Mountain have also been summarized by Lindsey and others (1973). The data, also summarized in table 5, come from both argillically and feldspathically altered mineralized tuffs, which contain some carbonate clasts. The mineralogy is dominated by clays, potassium feldspar, quartz, and cristobalite. Calcite and dolomite clasts are locally important. Fluorite is locally abundant in the ore assemblages and bertrandite is an important trace mineral. Uranium does not form discrete phases but instead is probably bound in fluorite and opal (Lindsey, 1981).

Acid-Base Accounting

Acid-base accounting data are lacking for the Spor Mountain deposit. Nevertheless, the lack of sulfide minerals and the presence of carbonate minerals as clasts suggest that the waste material should be net-alkaline in character.

Element Mobility Related to Mining in Groundwater and Surface Water

The only site-specific data for groundwater associated with a Spor Mountain-type deposit are the results of Bolke and Sumsion (1978) from the lone well sampled at the site in 1977, roughly eight years after the start of mining. The well was within the rhyolite and reached a depth of approximately 190 m. The geochemical characteristics of the groundwater at the mine site are compared to other groundwater samples in the study area in table 7. The pH was not measured at the time of sampling, but the major-element chemistry, including fluoride concentrations, was similar to that of the regional groundwater sampled at two sites within 10 km of the mine (table 7).

Ecosystem Issues

Ecosystem issues related to mining are unlikely in the vicinity of the Spor Mountain deposits because of the arid climate, lack of surface water, and the low concentrations of beryllium and uranium in the ores. Water-quality criteria for beryllium are currently lacking in the United States. However, USEPA (1980) does provide lowest observable effects limits as guidance for acute and chronic toxicity to aquatic life for Be of 130 and 5.3 µg/L, respectively. Water hardness is reported to have a significant effect on the acute toxicity of Be (USEPA, 1980). In contrast, LeBlanc (1980) determined lethal concentrations for 50 percent of test organisms (LC_{50}) for *Daphnia magna* of 1,900 µg/L for 24-hour exposures, and

1,000 µg/L for 48-hour exposures in test water with a hardness of 173 mg/L $CaCO_3$ and pH 8. Jagoe and others (1993) found acute toxicity (mortality) to juvenile perch (*Perca fluviatlis*) at dissolved Be concentrations greater than 10 µg/L at pH 4.5 and greater than 50 µg/L at pH 5.5; concentrations greater than 100 µg/L were lethal to juvenile roach (*Rutilus rutilus*) regardless of pH. Relative to bertrandite solubility, these concentrations would only be expected below a pH of 3 (fig. 17). Sediment guidelines are lacking for Be.

The ecological toxicity of Be in soils has been assessed by Kuperman and others (2006) who investigated chronic effects on soil invertebrates, such as earthworms, potworms, and collembola by dose-response assessment methods. Their lowest measured value of no-observed-effect concentration was 18 mg/kg, and their lowest lowest-observed-effect concentration for a survival endpoint was 24 mg/kg. Their lowest value of no-observed-effect concentration for a reproduction endpoint was 24 mg/kg, and their lowest value of lowest-observed-effect concentration was 36 mg/kg.

Human Health Issues

Human health concerns associated with Spor Mountain-type Be deposits and their wastes center around airborne particulates at ore-processing facilities. Beryllium concentrations in excess of the drinking water standard (4 µg/L; table 8) are unlikely due to the low solubility of bertrandite (fig. 17).

Several studies have investigated Be toxicity associated with the mining and milling of ores at Spor Mountain (Deubner and others, 2001; Stefaniak and others, 2008). In addition, a review of the health effects of Be was conducted by the U.S. National Research Council (2007). A major concern is "chronic Be disease," which is a debilitating and potentially lethal lung disease, and its precursor, Be sensitization, an immune system disorder, both of which are most commonly described from the nuclear weapons and Be manufacturing industries via an inhalation pathway (Kreiss and others, 2007). Also, the United States Environmental Protection Agency classifies Be as a likely human carcinogen (U.S. National Research Council, 2007). Neither Be sensitization nor chronic Be disease have been diagnosed in miners at Spor Mountain (Deubner and others, 2001), which is consistent with the low Be concentrations of the ores being mined. Deubner and others (2001) found median breathing zone and lapel air-sample concentrations associated with mining and milling at Spor Mountain to be less than 0.8 micrograms per cubic meter (µg/m^3) over their monitoring period from 1971 to 1999, compared to the threshold level value of 2 µg/m^3 (table 9). They also suggested that the speciation of Be in solid form may affect its toxicity, with bertrandite, beryl, and Be salts posing lower risks than Be hydroxide.

Climate Effects on Geoenvironmental Signatures

Studies related to climatic effects on geoenvironmental signatures on volcanogenic Be deposits are lacking. Nevertheless, the absence of significant secondary Be salts, the low solubility of bertrandite and fluorite, and the low but significant concentrations of uranium associated with the ores suggest that climatic variations should not greatly influence the geochemical behavior of Be or associated fluorine and uranium.

Exploration and Resource Assessment Guides

1. Rhyolitic rocks rich in fluorine, beryllium, tin, and other lithophile metals are the favorable volcanic-magmatic source for these deposits. Beryllium tuffs are genetically related to volcanic and hypabyssal biotite-bearing topaz rhyolites and ongonites. The regional character of the associated igneous suites is bimodal and can consist of a broad compositional array from peraluminous to peralkaline igneous rocks, although the immediate host volcanic rocks are typically weakly peraluminous to metaluminous in composition. In the Western United States, these rocks are mostly plugs, domes, flows, and tuffs of Tertiary topaz-bearing rhyolite.

2. Deep fractures, such as margin faults and caldera ring fractures related to extensional tectonics, are instrumental in tapping the sources of rhyolitic magma and lithophile-rich mineralizing fluids. The process of magma mixing is thought to provide the primary mechanism for explosive volcanism, as is supported by geochemical attributes of the volcanic system, mafic inclusions, vent structures, and volcaniclastic surge deposits.

3. Porous carbonate-bearing tuffs and vitric volcaniclastic rocks are favorable hosts for volcanogenic Be deposits. The reactive carbonate minerals may occur as lithic fragments, veins, and (or) disseminations in tuff. The richest Be ore zones may be associated with mineralized carbonate lithic-rich phreatomagmatic base surge deposits, or other carbonate lithic-rich volcanic units. Adjacent breccia zones in carbonate rocks may also provide suitable host rocks for localized deposits.

4. Fluorspar and uranium deposits indicate the presence of lithophile-rich mineralizing hydrothermal fluids capable of transporting economic amounts of Be. General estimates of temperatures of formation of volcanogenic Be deposits are between 100°C and 200°C based on fluid data, low-temperature mineralogy (bertrandite versus phenakite), and cryptocrystalline grain size.

5. A distinctive association of hydrothermal alteration minerals is a favorable indicator of proximity to volcanogenic Be deposits. Alteration processes related to Be-mineralization can be expected to result in widespread and pervasive hydrothermal alteration haloes of smectite, sericite, and potassium feldspar. The presence of abundant trioctahedral lithium smectite, which forms early as magnesium becomes available from alteration of dolomite and as Li, Zn, U, Th, and Mn are supplied by mineralizing solutions, is a particularly favorable indicator.

6. Anomalous concentrations of Be, Ce, F, Ga, Li, Nb, and Y in otherwise unaltered volcanic rocks may also indicate favorability for volcanogenic Be deposits. These elements define primary dispersion halos that act as vectors to Be ore. Geochemical halos may extend as far as 3–4 km into unaltered tuff. Thus, the halos form a target on the order of 156 km^2 that may be expected to enclose volcanogenic Be deposits covering ≈52 km^2

7. Economic volcanogenic Be districts are likely to be made up of many small mineralized lenses that, as a whole, may cover 50 km^2 or more, but that individually may cover only 100s of square meters.

Acknowledgments

Chemical analyses of melt inclusions were conducted in the Denver Inclusion Analysis Lab (DIAL) by David Adams, Todor Todorov, and Erin Marsh. The ^{40}Ar-^{39}Ar analyses on sanidine and resulting isotopic dates were conducted by Mike Cosca and John Lee. The report has benefitted greatly from constructive and thoughtful reviews by Virginia McLemore (New Mexico Bureau of Geology and Mineral Resources), Donald Burt (Arizona State University), and Richard Goldfarb (U.S. Geological Survey).

References Cited

Adams, D.T., Hofstra, A.H., Cosca, M.A., Todorov, T.I., and Marsh, E.E., 2009, Age of sanidine and composition of melt inclusions in quartz phenocrysts from volcanic rocks associated with large Mo and Be deposits in the Western United States [abs.]: Geological Society of America Annual Meeting, Abstracts with Programs, vol. 41, no. 7, p. 255.

Alexsandrov, S.M., 2010, Skarn-greisen deposits of the Lost River and Mount Ear ore field, Seward Peninsula, Alaska, United States: Geochemistry International, v. 48, no. 12, p. 1220–1236.

Baker, J.M., Keith, J.D., Christiansen, E.H., Griffen, D.T., Tingey, D.G., and Dorais, M.J., 1998, Genesis of red beryl in topaz rhyolites, Thomas Range, Utah [abs.]: Geological Society of America Abstracts with Program, v. 30, p. 370–371.

Ball, J.W., and Nordstrom, D.K., 1991, User's manual for WATEQ4F, with revised thermodynamic data base and test cases for calculation speciation of major, trace, and redox elements in natural waters: U.S. Geological Survey Open-File Report 91–183, 188 p.

Barton, M.D., 1986, Phase equilibria and thermodynamic properties of minerals in the $BeO-Al_2O_3-SiO_2-H_2O$ (BASH) system, with petrologic applications: American Mineralogist, v. 71, p. 277–300.

Barton, M.D., and Young, Steven, 2002, Non-pegmatitic deposits of beryllium: Mineralogy, geology, phase equilibria and origin, in Grew, E.S., ed., Beryllium: Mineralogy, petrology and geochemistry: Reviews in Mineralogy and Geochemistry, v. 50, p. 591–691.

Best, M.G., McKee, E.H., and Damon, P.E., 1980, Spacetime + composition patterns of late Cenozoic mafic volcanism, southwestern Utah and adjoining areas: American Journal of Science, v. 280, p. 1035–1050.

Beus, A.A., 1966, Geochemistry of beryllium and genetic types of beryllium deposits: San Francisco, W.H. Freeman, 401 p.

Bikun, J.V., 1980, Fluorine and lithophile element mineralization at Spor Mountain, Utah: U.S. Department of Energy Open-File Report GJBX-225(80), p. 167–376.

Bolke, E.L., and Sumsion, C.T., 1978, Hydrologic reconnaissance of the Fish Springs Flat area, Tooele, Juab, and Millard Counties, Utah: State of Utah Department of Natural Resources Technical Publication No. 64, 30 p.

Bowyer, Ben, 1963, Yellow Chief uranium mine, Juab County, Utah, in Sharp, B.J., and Williams, N.C., eds., Beryllium and uranium mineralization in western Juab County, Utah: Utah Geological Society Guidebook to the Geology of Utah, no. 17, p. 15–22.

Breit, G.N., and Hall, S.M., 2011, Deposit model for volcanogenic uranium deposits: U.S. Geological Survey Open-File Report 2011–1255, 5 p.

Brush Engineered Materials, Inc., 2009, Transforming our world and yours: Annual report, 122 p., accessed May 15, 2012, at *http://files.shareholder.com/downloads/ BW/1857629296x0x368575/A9F177AF-D3E5-4546-8707- 73F26F14E146/bw2009ar.pdf.*

Bullock, K.C., 1981, Geology of the fluorite occurrences, Spor Mountain, Juab County, Utah: Utah Geological and Mineral Survey Special Studies 53, 31p.

Burt, D.M., and Sheridan, M.F., 1981, Model for the formation of uranium/lithophile element deposits in fluorine-rich volcanic rocks, in Goodell, P.C., and Waters, A.C., eds., Uranium in volcanic and volcaniclastic rocks: American Association of Petroleum Geologists Studies in Geology 13, p. 99–109.

Burt, D.M., and Sheridan, M.F., 1986, Mineral deposits related to topaz rhyolites in the Southwest: Arizona Geological Society Digest, v. 16, p. 170–178.

Burt, D.M., and Sheridan, M.F., 1988, Mineralization associated with topaz rhyolites and related rocks in Mexico, in Taylor, R.P., and Strong, D.F., eds., Recent advances in the geology of granite-related mineral deposits: Canadian Institute of Mining and Metallurgy Special Paper 39, p. 303–306.

Burt, D.M., Bikun, J.V., and Christiansen, E.H., 1982, Topaz rhyolites: Distribution, origin, and significance for exploration: Economic Geology, v. 77, p. 1818–1836.

Burt, D.M., Knauth, L.P., Wohletz, K.H., and Sheridan, M.F., 2008, Surge deposit misidentification at Spor Mountain, Utah and elsewhere: A cautionary message for Mars: Journal of Volcanology and Geothermal Research, v. 177, p. 755–759.

Canadian Council of Ministers of the Environment (CCME), 2007, Canadian soil quality guidelines for the protection of environmental and human health: Uranium (2007), in Canadian environmental quality guidelines, 1999: Winnipeg, Canadian Council of Ministers of the Environment, 14 p., available at *http://ceqg-rcqe.ccme.ca/.*

Canadian Council of Ministers of the Environment (CCME), 2010, Guidelines for Canadian drinking water quality summary table, in Canadian environmental quality guidelines: Prepared by the Federal-Provincial-Territorial Committee on Drinking Water Health Canada, 14 p., available at *http://ceqg-rcqe.ccme.ca/.*

Christiansen, R.L., and Lipman, P.W., 1972, Cenozoic volcanism and plate tectonic evolution of the Western United States; II, Late Cenozoic: Philosophical Transactions of the Royal Society of London, Series A, 271, p. 249–284.

Christiansen, E.H., and Venchiarutti, D.A., 1990, Magmatic inclusions in rhyolites of the Spor Mountain Formation, western Utah: Limitations on compositional inferences from inclusions in granitic rocks: Journal of Geophysical Research, v. 95, p. 17717–17728.

Christiansen, E.H., Bikun, J.V., Sheridan, M.F., and Burt, D.M., 1984, Geochemical evolution of topaz rhyolites from the Thomas Range and Spor Mountain, Utah: American Mineralogist, v. 69, p. 223–236.

Christiansen, E.H., Burt, D.M., and Sheridan, M.F., 1986, The geology of topaz rhyolites from the Western United States: Geological Society of America Special Paper 205, 82 p.

Christiansen, E.H., Burt, D.M., Sheridan, M.F., and Wilson, R.T., 1983, Petrogenesis of topaz rhyolites: Contributions to Mineralogy and Petrology, v. 83, p. 16–30.

Christiansen, E.H., Haapala, Iimari, and Hart, G.L., 2007, Are Cenozoic topaz rhyolites the erupted equivalents of Protero-zoic rapakivi granites? Examples from the Western United States and Finland: Lithos, v. 97, p. 219–246.

Christiansen, E.H., Keith, J.D., and Thompson, T.J., 1997, Origin of gem red beryl in the Wah Wah Mountains, Utah: Mining Engineering, v. 49, p. 37–41.

Christiansen, E.H., Stuckless, J.S., Funkhouser, M.M.J., Howell, K.H., 1988, Petrogenesis of rare-metal granites from depleted crustal sources: An example from the Cenozoic of western Utah, U.S.A., *in* Taylor, R.P., and Strong, D.F., eds., Recent advances in the geology of granite-related mineral deposits: Canadian Institute of Mining and Metallurgy Special Paper 39, p. 307–321.

Congdon, R.D., and Nash, W.P., 1991, Eruptive pegmatite magma: Rhyolite of the Honey Comb Hills, Utah: American Mineralogist, v. 76, p. 1261–1278.

Deubner, David, Kelsh, Michael, Shum, Mona, Maier, Lisa, Kent, Michael, and Lau, Edmund, 2001, Beryllium sensiti-zation, chronic beryllium disease, and exposures at a beryl-lium mining and extraction facility: Applied Occupational and Environmental Hygiene, v. 16, no. 5, p. 579–592.

Dietrich, A., Lehmann, B., and Wallianos, A., 2000, Bulk rock and melt inclusion geochemistry of Bolivian tin porphyry systems: Economic Geology, v. 95, p. 313–326.

Donahue, K.M., 2002, Geochemistry, geology and geochro-nology of the Victorio mining district, Luna County, New Mexico: Linking skarn and porphyry systems to carbonate-hosted lead-zinc replacement deposits: Socorro, New Mexico Institute of Mining and Technology, M.S. thesis, 195 p., available at *http://ees.nmt.edu/alumni/papers/2002t_donahue_km.pd; accessed December 12, 2011f.*

Duffield, W.A., and Dalrymple, G.B., 1990, The Taylor Creek Rhyolite of New Mexico; a rapidly emplaced field of lava domes and flows: Bulletin of Volcanology v. 52, p. 475–487.

Eby, G.N., 1992, Chemical subdivisions of the A-type granit-oids; petrogenetic and tectonic implications: Geology, v. 20, p. 641–644.

Grew, E.S., 2002, Mineralogy, petrology and geochemistry of beryllium: An introduction and list of beryllium minerals, *in* Grew, E.S., ed., Beryllium—Mineralogy, petrology, and geochemistry: Reviews in Mineralogy and Geochemistry, v. 50, p. 1–49.

Griffitts, W.R.,1964, Beryllium, *in* Mineral and water resources of Utah: Utah Geological and Mineralogical Survey Bulletin 73, p. 71–75.

Griffitts, W.R., 1965, Recently discovered beryllium deposits near Gold Hill, Utah: Economic Geology, v. 60, p. 1298–1305.

Griffitts, W.R., and Cooley, E.F., 1978, A beryllium-fluorite survey at Aguachile Mountain, Coahuila, Mexico: Journal of Geochemical Exploration, v. 9, p. 137–147.

Griffitts, W.R., and Rader, L.F., 1963, Beryllium and fluorine in mineralized tuff, Spor Mountain, Juab County, Utah: U.S. Geological Survey Professional Paper 475–B, p. B16–B17.

Hattori, K., and Keith, J.D., 2001, Contribution of mafic melt to porphyry copper mineralization: Evidence from Mount Pinatubo, Philippines, and Bingham Canyon, Utah, USA: Mineralium Deposita, v. 36, p. 799–806.

Hawkins, Greg, 2001, Open pit surgical mining of bertrandite ores at the world's largest beryllium deposit!, *in* Simandl, G.J., Holland, Janet, Dunlop, Susan, and Rotella, M.D., eds., 2001 industrial minerals in Canada; Program and extended abstracts for the 37th forum on the geology of industrial minerals: Forum on the Geology of Industrial Minerals, v. 37, p. 105–106.

Henry, C.D., 1992, Beryllium and other rare metals in Trans-Pecos, Texas: Bulletin West Texas Geological Society, v. 31, p. 1–15.

Hillard, P.D., 1969, Geology and beryllium mineralization near Apache Warm Springs, Socorro County, New Mexico: New Mexico Bureau of Mines and Mineral Resources Circular 103, 16 p.

Jagoe, C.H., Matey, V.E., Haines, T.A., and Komov, V.T., 1993, Effect of beryllium on fish in acid water is analogous to aluminum toxicity: Aquatic Toxicology, v. 24, p. 241–256.

Jaskula, B.W., 2010, Beryllium: U.S. Geological Survey Mineral Commodity Summaries, Mineral Yearbook—2011, p. 28–29.

Johnson, T.W., and Ripley, E.M., 1998, Hydrogen and oxygen isotopic systematics of beryllium mineralization, Spor Mountain, Utah [abs]: Geological Society of America Abstracts with Program, v. 30, p. A-127.

Kamilli, R.J., Ludington, Steve, and Plumlee, G.S., in press, Alkali-feldspar rhyolite-granite (AFRG) porphyry molybdenum deposits: U.S. Geological Survey Scientific Investigations Report.

Keith, J.D., Christiansen, E.H., and Tingey, D.G., 1994, Geological and chemical conditions of formation of red beryl, Wah Wah Mountains, Utah: Utah Geological Association Publication, no. 23, p. 155–170.

Kesler, S.E., 1977, Geochemistry of manto fluorite deposits, northern Coahuila, Mexico: Economic Geology, v. 72, no. 2, p. 204–218.

Kesler, S.E., Ruiz, Joaquin., and Jones, L.M., 1983, Strontium-isotopic geochemistry of fluorite mineralization (Coahuila, Mexico): Chemical Geology, v. 41, p. 65–75.

Kim, S.K., 2010, Cost-benefit analysis of BeO-UO$_2$ nuclear fuel: Elsevier, Progress in Nuclear Energy, v. 52, issue 8, p. 813–821, available at *http://www.sciencedirect.com/science/article/pii/S0149197010001101.*

Kovalenko, V.I., and Kovalenko, N.I., 1976, Ongonites (topaz bearing quartz keratophyre)—Subvolcanic analogue of rare metal Li-F granites (in Russian): Nauka Press, Moscow, 125 p.

Kovalenko, V.I., Samoylov, V.S., and Goreglyad, A.V., 1979, Volcanic ongonites enriched in rare elements: Transactions USSR Academy of Science (Earth Science Section) v. 246, p. 58–61.

Kovalenko, V.I., and Yarmolyuk, V.V., 1995, Endogenous rare metal ore formations and rare metal metallogeny of Mongolia: Economic Geology, v. 90, p. 520–529.

Kreiss, Kathleen., Day, G.A., and Schuler, C.R., 2007, Beryllium: A modern industrial hazard?: Annual Review of Public Health, v. 28, p. 259–277.

Kremenetsky, A.A., Beskin, S.M., Lehmann, B., and Seltmann, R., 2000, Economic geology of granite-related ore deposits of Russia and other FSU countries: An overview, *in* Kremenetsky A.A., Lehmann B., and Seltmann R., eds., Ore-bearing granites of Russia and adjacent countries: IGCP Project 373, IMGRE, Moscow, p. 3–60.

Kuperman, R.G., Checkai, R.T., Simini, M.A., Phillips, C.T., Speicher, J.A., and Barclift, D.J., 2006, Toxicity benchmarks for antimony, barium, and beryllium determined using reproduction endpoints for Folsomia candida, *Eisenia fetida*, and *Enchytraeus crypticus*: Environmental Toxicology and Chemistry, v. 25, no. 3, p. 754–762.

LeBlanc, G.A., 1980, Acute toxicity of priority pollutants to water flea (*Daphnia magna*): Bulletin of Environmental Contamination and Toxicology, v. 24, p. 684–691.

Lehmann, Bernd, Ishihara, Shunso, Michel, Hubert, Miller, Jim, Rapela, C.W., Sanchez, Alberto, Tistl, Michael, and Winkelmann, Lothar, 1990, The Bolivian tin province and regional tin distribution in the Central Andes: A reassessment: Economic Geology, v. 85, p. 1044–1058.

Levinson, A.A., 1962, Beryllium-fluorite mineralization at Aguachile Mountain, Coahuila, Mexico: American Mineralogist, v. 47, p. 67–74.

Lin, Desong, 1985, A preliminary study on genesis of an altered volcanic type beryl deposit in South China: Mineral Deposits, v. 3, available at *http://en.cnki.com.cn/Article_en/CJFDTOTAL-KCDZ198503002.htm.*

Lin, Yin., Pollard, P.J., Hu, Shoixi, and Taylor, R.G., 1995, Geologic and geochemical characteristics of the Yichun Ta-Nb-Li deposit, Jiangxi Province, South China: Economic Geology, v. 90, p. 577–585.

Lindsey, D.A., 1973, Mineralogical and chemical data for alteration studies, Spor Mountain beryllium deposits, Juab County, Utah: U.S. Geological Survey Report 31, available from U.S. Department of Commerce National Technical Information Service, Springfield, Va., as report PB-220-552, 24 p.

Lindsey, D.A., 1975, Mineralization halos and diagenesis in water-laid tuff of the Thomas Range, Utah: U.S. Geological Survey Professional Paper 818–B, p. B1–B19.

Lindsey, D.A., 1977, Epithermal beryllium deposits in water-laid tuff, western Utah: Economic Geology v. 72, p. 219–232.

Lindsey, D.A., 1978, Geology of the Yellow Chief mine, Thomas Range, Juab County, Utah, *in* Shawe, D.R., ed., Guidebook to mineral deposits of the Great Basin: Nevada Bureau of Mines and Geology Report 32, p. 65–68.

Lindsey, D.A., 1979a, Preliminary report on Tertiary volcanism and uranium mineralization in the Thomas Range and northern Drum Mountains, Juab County, Utah: U.S. Geological Survey Open-File Report 79–1076, 101 p.

Lindsey, D.A., 1979b, Geologic map and cross-sections of Tertiary rocks in the Thomas Range and northern Drum Mountains, Juab County, Utah: U.S. Geological Survey Miscellaneous Investigations Map I–1176, scale 1:62,500.

Lindsey, D.A., 1981, Volcanism and uranium mineralization at Spor Mountain, Utah, *in* Goodell, P.C., and Waters, A.C., eds., Uranium in volcanic and volcaniclastic rocks: American Association of Petroleum Geology Studies in Geology No. 13, p. 89–98.

Lindsey, D.A., 1982, Tertiary volcanic rocks and uranium in the Thomas Range and northern Drum Mountains, Juab County, Utah: U. S. Geological Survey Professional Paper 1221, 71 p.

Lindsey, D.A., 1998, Slides of the fluorspar, beryllium, and uranium deposits at Spor Mountain, Utah: U.S. Geological Survey Open-File Report 98–524, [unpaged], available at *http://pubs.usgs.gov/of/1998/ofr-98-0524/*.

Lindsey, D.A., 2001, Beryllium deposits at Spor Mountain, Utah, *in* Bon, R.L., Riordan, R.F., Tripp, B.T., and Krukowski, S.T., eds., Proceedings of the 35th forum on the geology of industrial minerals; the Intermountain West forum 1999: Utah Geological Survey Report Miscellaneous Publication 01–2, p. 73–78.

Lindsey, D.A., Ganow, Harold, and Mountjoy, Wayne, 1973, Hydrothermal alteration associated with beryllium deposits at Spor Mountain, Utah: U.S. Geological Survey Professional Paper 818–A, p. A1–A20.

Lindsey, D.A., Naeser, C.R., and Shawe, D.R., 1975, Age of volcanism and mineralization in the Thomas Range, Keg Mountain, and Desert Mountain, western Utah: U.S. Geological Survey Journal of Research, v. 3, p. 75–597.

Lipman, P.W., Rowley, P.D., Mehnert, H.H., Evans, S.H., Nash, W.P., and Brown, F.H., 1978, Pleistocene rhyolite of the Mineral Mountains, Utah: Geothermal and archeological significance: U.S. Geological Survey Journal of Research, v. 6, p. 133–147.

Loiselle, M.C., and Wones, D.R., 1979, Characteristics and origin of anorogenic granites [abs.]: Geological Society of America, Abstracts with Programs, v. 11, p. 468.

Ludington, Steve, and Plumlee, G.S., 2009, Climax-type porphyry molybdenum deposits: U.S. Geological Survey Open-File Report 2009–1215, 16 p.

Ludwig, K.R., Lindsey, D.A., Zielinski, R.A., and Simmons, K.R., 1980, U-Pb ages of uraniferous opals and implications for the history of beryllium, fluorine, and uranium mineralization at Spor Mountain, Utah: Earth and Planetary Science Letters, v. 46, p. 221–232.

Lykhin, D.A. Kovalenko, V.I., Yarmolyuk, V.V., Kotov, A.B., Kovach, V.P., and Sal'nikova, E. B., 2004, Age, composition, and sources of ore-bearing magmatism of the Orot beryllium deposit in western Transbaikalia, Russia [abs.]: Pleiades Publishing, Ltd. (Плеадес Паблишинг, Лтд), Geology of Ore Deposits, available at *http://www.maik.ru/ cgi-perl/search.pl?type=abstract&name=geolore&number =2&year=4&page=108*.

Lykhin, D.A., Kovalenko, V.I., Yarmolyuk, V.V., Sal'nikova, E.B., Kotov, A.B., Anisimova, I.V., and Plotkina, Yu.V., 2010, The Yermakovsky beryllium deposit, western Transbaikal region, Russia: Geochronology of igneous rocks: Pleiades Publishing, Ltd., Geology of Ore Deposits, v. 52, no. 2, p. 114–137 (originally published in Geologiya Rudnykh Mestorozhdenii, 2010, v. 52, no. 2, p. 126–152).

Materion Corporation, 2011, Brush performance alloys: Materion Corporation Web site accessed July 13, 2011, at *http://materion.com/Businesses/Brush%20Performance%20 Alloys/Products.aspx*.

McAnulty, W.N., and Levinson, A.A., 1964, Rare alkali and beryllium mineralization in volcanic tuffs, Honey Comb Hills, Juab County, Utah: Economic Geology, v. 59, no. 5, p. 768–774.

McAnulty, W.N., Sewell, C.R., Atkinson, D.R., and Rasberry, J.M., 1963, Aquachile beryllium-bearing fluorspar district, Coahuila, Mexico: Geological Society of America Bulletin, v. 74, p. 735–744.

McLemore, V.T., 2010a, Beryllium deposits in New Mexico and adjacent areas, including evaluation of the NURE stream sediment data: New Mexico Bureau of Geology and Mineral Resources Open-File Report OF–533, 105 p., available at *http://geoinfo.nmt.edu/publications/openfile/details. cfml?Volume=533*.

McLemore, V.T., 2010b, Geology, mineral resources, and geoarchaeology of the Montoya Butte quadrangle, including the Ojo Caliente No. 2 mining district, Socorro County, New Mexico: New Mexico Bureau of Geology and Mineral Resources Open-File Report OF–535, 200 p.

Meeves, H.C., 1966, Nonpegmatitic beryllium occurrences in Arizona, Colorado, New Mexico, Utah, and four adjacent States: U.S. Bureau of Mines Report of Investigations 6828, 68 p.

Montoya, J.W., Baur, G.S., and Wilson, S.R., 1964, Mineralogical investigations of beryllium-bearing tuff, Honey Comb Hills, Juab County, Utah: U.S. Bureau of Mines Report of Investigations 6408, 11 p.

Montoya, J.W., Havens, R.J., and Bridges, D.W., 1962, Beryllium-bearing tuff from Spot Mountain, Utah: Its chemical, mineralogical and physical properties: U.S. Bureau of Mines Report of Investigations 6084, 15 p.

Morad, S., Ketzer, J.M., and De Ros, L.F., 2000, Spatial and temporal distribution of diagenetic alterations in siliciclastic rocks: Implications for mass transfer in sedimentary basins: Sedimentology, v. 4.47, (Suppl.1), p. 95–120.

Murphy, B.A., 1980, Studies of mineralization at Spor Mountain, Utah, and a comprehensive Spor Mountain bibliography: U.S. Department of Energy Open-File Report GJBX-225(80), p. 378–414.

Nash, J.T, 2010, Volcanogenic uranium deposits: Geology, geochemical processes, and criteria for resource assessment: U.S. Geological Survey Open-File Report 2010–1001, 99 p.

National Institute of Occupational Safety and Health (NIOSH), 2005, NIOSH pocket guide to chemical hazards: NIOSH Publication Number 2005-149, available at *http://www.cdc.gov/niosh/npg/default.html.*

Nkambule, M.V., 1988, Skarn mineralization at Iron Mountain, New Mexico, in light of fluid inclusion studies: Socorro, New Mexico Institute of Mining and Technology, M.S. thesis, 56 p., available at *http://ees.nmt.edu/alumni/papers/1988t_nkambule_mv.pdf.*

Noble, S.R., Spooner, E.T.C., and Harris, F.R., 1984, The Logtung large tonnage, low-grade tungsten (scheelite)-molybdenum porphyry deposit, south-central Yukon Territory: Economic Geology, v. 79, p. 848–868.

Park, G.M., 2006, Fluorspar, uranium, and beryllium deposits at Spor Mountain and historical overview of the discovery and geology of the Topaz Mountains, Utah, *in* Bon, R.L., Gloyn, R.W., and Park, G.M., eds., Mining districts of Utah: Utah Geological Association Publication 32, p. 565–593.

Pichavant, Michel, Kontak, D.J., Briqueu, L.A., Valencia, H.J., and Clark, A.H., 1988a, The Miocene-Pliocene Macusani Volcanics, SE Peru: 2, Geochemistry and origin of a felsic peraluminous magma: Contributions to Mineralogy and Petrology, v. 100, p. 325–338.

Pichavant, Michel, Kontak, D.J., Valencia, H.J., and Clark, A.H. 1988b, The Miocene-Pliocene Macusani Volcanics, SE Peru: 1, Mineralogy and magmatic evolution of a two-mica aluminosilicate-bearing ignimbrite suite: Contributions to Mineralogy and Petrology, v. 100, p. 300–324.

Price, J.G., Rubin, J.N., Henry, C.D., Pinkston, T.L., Tweedy, S.W., and Koppenaal, D.W., 1990, Rare-metal enriched peraluminous rhyolites in a continental arc, Sierra Blanca area, Trans-Pecos Texas: Chemical modification by vapor-phase crystallization, *in* Stein, H.J., and Hannah, J.L., eds., Ore-bearing granite systems: Petrogenesis and mineralizing processes: Geological Society of America Special Paper 246, p. 103–120.

Ramsden, A.R., French, D.H., and Chalmers, D.I., 1993, Volcanic-hosted rare-metals deposit at Brockman, Western Australia: Mineralogy and geochemistry of the Niobium tuff: Mineral Deposita, v. 28, p. 1–12.

Reyf, F.G., 2008, Alkali granite and Be (phenakite–bertrandite) mineralization at the Orot and Yermakovka deposits: Geokhimiya, v. 46, no. 3, p. 243–263 [Geochemistry International, v. 46, no. 3, p. 213–232 (2008)].

Reyf, F.G., and Ishkov, Y.M., 2006, Be-bearing sulfate-fluoride brines, a product of residual pegmatite's distillation within the alkaline granite intrusion (the Yermakova F-Be deposit, Transbaikalia): Geokhimiya, v. 44, p. 1096–1111. [2006 translation, originally published in 1999 in Russian, Geochemistry International v. 37, p. 985–999.]

Richardson, C.K., and Holland, H.D., 1979, Fluorite deposition in hydrothermal systems: Geochimica Cosmochimica Acta, v. 43, p. 1327–1335.

Rimstidt, J.D., 1997, Chapter 10. Gangue mineral transport and deposition, *in* Barnes, H.L., ed., Geochemistry of hydrothermal ore deposits (3rd ed.): New York, Wiley, p. 487–515.

Rodionov, S.M., 2000, Tin metallogeny of the Russian Far East: Ore-bearing granites of Russia and adjacent countries: Moscow, Institut Mineralogii, Geokhimii I Kristallokhimii, Academy of Sciences of the USSR, p. 234–262.

Rowan, L.C., and Mars, J.C., 2003, Lithologic mapping in the Mountain Pass, California, area using advanced spaceborne thermal emission and reflection radiometer (ASTER) data: Remote Sensing of Environment, v. 84, p. 350–366.

Rubin, J.N., Price, J.G., Henry, C.D., and Koppenaal, D.W., 1987, Cryolite-bearing and rare metal-enriched rhyolite, Sierra Blanca Peaks, Hudspeth County, Texas: American Mineralogist, v. 72, p. 1122–1130.

Rubin, J.N., Price, J.G., Henry, C.D., Pinkston, T.L., Tweedy, S.W., Koppenaal, D.W., Peterson, S.B., Harlan, H.M., Miller, W.T., Thompson, R.J., Grabowski, R.B., Laybourn, D.P., Schrock, G.E., Johnson, A., Staes, D.G., Gaines, R.V., and Miller, F.H., 1988, Mineralogy of beryllium deposits at Sierra Blanca, Texas, *in* Torma, A.E, and Gundiler, I.H., eds., Precious and rare metal technologies: Amsterdam, Elsevier, Proceedings; Symposium on Precious and Rare Metals, Albuquerque, N. Mex., p. 601–614.

Rubin, J.N., Price, J.G., Henry, C.D., and Kyle, J.R., 1990, Geology of beryllium-rare earth element deposits near Sierra Blanca, Texas: Society of Economic Geologists Field Trip Guidebook, 1990 Annual Meeting, Dallas, 10 p.

Sainsbury, C.L., 1964, Association of beryllium with tin deposits rich in fluorite: Economic Geology, v. 59, p. 920–929.

Shacklette, H.T., and Boerngen, J.G., 1984, Elemental concentrations in soils and other surficial materials of the conterminous United States: U.S. Geological Survey Professional Paper 1270, 105 p.

Shawe, D.R., 1966, Arizona–New Mexico and Nevada–Utah beryllium belt: U.S. Geological Survey Professional Paper 550–C, 206–213.

Shawe, D.R., 1968, Geology of the Spor Mountain beryllium district, Utah, *in* Ridge, J.D., ed., Ore deposits of the United States, 1933–1967 (Graton-Sales volume): New York, American Institute of Mining, Metallurgical, and Petroleum Engineers, v. 2, pt. 8, p. 1149–1161.

Shawe, D.R., 1972, Reconnaissance geology and mineral potential of the Thomas, Keg, and Desert calderas, central Juab County, Utah: U.S. Geological Survey Professional Paper 800–B, p. B67–B77.

Simpkins, T.H., 1983, Geology and geochemistry of the Agua-chile Mountain fluorspar-beryllium mining district, northern Coahuila, Mexico: Alpine, Tex., Sul Ross State University, M.S. thesis, 137 p.

Singer, D.A., and Berger, V.I., 2007, Deposit models and their application in mineral resource assessment, *in* Briskey, J.A., and Schulz, K.J., eds., Proceedings for a workshop on deposit modeling, mineral resource assessment, and their role in sustainable development: U.S. Geological Survey Circular 1294, 143 p., available at *http://pubs.usgs.gov/circ/2007/1294/*.

Sparks, S.J.R., Sigurdsson, Harald, and Wilson, Lionel, 1977, Magma mixing: A mechanism for triggering acid explosive eruptions: Nature, v. 267, p. 315–318.

Staatz, M.H., 1963, Geology of the beryllium deposits in the Thomas Range, Juab County, Utah: U.S. Geological Survey Bulletin, 1142–M, 36 p.

Staatz, M.H., and Carr, W.J., 1964, Geology and mineral deposits of the Thomas and Dugway Ranges, Juab and Tooele Counties, Utah: U.S. Geological Survey Professional Paper 415, 188 p.

Staatz, M.H., and Griffitts, W.R., 1961, Beryllium-bearing tuff in the Thomas Range, Juab County, Utah: Economic Geology, v. 56, p. 941–950.

Staatz, M.H., and Osterwald, F.W., 1959, Geology of the Thomas Range fluorspar district, Juab County, Utah: U.S. Geological Survey Bulletin 1069, 97 p.

Stefaniak, A.B., Chipera, S.J., Day, G.A., Sabey, P.L., Dickerson, R.M., Sbarra, D.C., Duling, M.G., Lawrence, R.B., Stanton, M.L., and Scripsick, R.C., 2008, Physicochemical characteristics of aerosol particles generated during the milling of beryllium silicate ores: Implications for risk assessment: Journal of Toxicology and Environmental Health, Part A., v. 71, p. 1468–1481.

Stonehouse, A.J., 1986, Physics and chemistry of beryllium: Journal of Vacuum Science and Technology A, v. 4, no. 3, p. 1163–1170.

Taylor, T.P., Ding, M.F., Ehler, D.S., Foreman, T.M., Kaszuba, J.P., and Sauer, N.N., 2003, Beryllium in the environment: A review: Journal of Environmental Science and Health, Part A—Toxic/Hazardous Substances and Environmental Engineering, v. A38, p. 439–469.

Taylor, W.R., Esslemont, G., Sun, S.S., 1995, Geology of the volcanic-hosted Brockman rare-metals deposit, Halls Creek mobile zone, Northwest Australia. II. Geochemistry and petrogenesis of the Brockman Volcanics: Mineralogy and Petrology, v. 52, p. 231–255.

Taylor, W.R., Page, R.W., Esslemont, G., Rock, N.M.S., and Chalmers, D.I., 1995, Geology of the volcanic-hosted Brockman rare-metals deposit, Halls Creek mobile zone, Northwest Australia. I. Volcanic environment, geochronology and petrography of the Brockman Volcanics: Mineralogy and Petrology v. 52, p. 209–230.

Thompson, T.J., Keith, J.D., Christiansen, E.H., Tingey, D.G., and Heizler, M.R., 1996, Genesis of topaz rhyolite hosted red beryl in the Wah Wah Mountains, Utah [abs]: Geological Society of America Abstracts with Programs, v. 28, p. A-154.

Tomberlin, T.A., 2004, Beryllium—A unique material in nuclear applications: 36th International SAMPLE Technical Conference, INEEL/CON-04-01869 Preprint [12] p.

Turley, C.P., and Nash, W.P., 1980, Petrology of late Tertiary and Quaternary volcanism in western Juab and Millard Counties, Utah: Utah Geological and Mineralogical Survey Special Study 52, p. l–33.

United States Environmental Protection Agency (USEPA), 1980, Ambient water quality criteria for beryllium: United States Environmental Protection Agency Web site, EPA 440 5-80-024 available at: *http://www.epa.gov/waterscience/criteria/library/ambientwqc/berryllium80.pdf.*

United States Environmental Protection Agency (USEPA), 2009, Regional screening level summary table: United States Environmental Protection Agency Web site, available at *http://www.epa.gov/region09/superfund/prg/index.html.*

United States National Research Council, Committee on Beryllium Alloy Exposures, 2007, Health effects of beryllium exposure: A literature review: Committee on Toxicology, National Research Council, 109 p., accessed July 12, 2011, at *http://www.nap.edu/catalog/12007.html.*

Veselý, Josef, Norton, S.A., Skrivan, Petr, Majer, Vladimir, Kram, Pavel, Navratil, Tomas, and Kaste, J.M., 2002, Environmental chemistry of beryllium, *in* Grew, E.S., ed., Beryllium; mineralogy, petrology, and geochemistry: Reviews in Mineralogy and Geochemistry, v. 50, p. 291–317.

Warner, L.A., Cameron, E.N., Holser, W.T., Wilmarth, V.R., and Cameron, E.M., 1959, Occurrence of nonpegmatite beryllium in the United States: U.S. Geological Survey Professional Paper 318, 198 p.

Webster, J.D., Holloway, J.R., and Hervig, R.L., 1989, Partitioning of lithophile trace elements between H_2O and H_2O + CO_2 fluids and topaz rhyolite melt: Economic Geology, v. 84, p. 116–134.

Wones, D.R., 1979, Intensive parameters during the crystallization of granitic plutons [abs.]: Geological Society of America, Abstracts with Programs, v. 11, p. 548.

Wood, S.A., 1992, Theoretical prediction of speciation and solubility of beryllium in hydrothermal solution to 300°C at saturated vapor pressure: Application to bertrandite/phenakite deposits: Ore Geology Reviews, v. 7, p. 249–278.

World Health Organization (WHO), 2008, Guidelines for drinking-water quality (3rd electronic version for the web): Geneva, Switzerland, WHO Press, available at *http://www.who.int/water_sanitation_health/dwq/gdwq3rev/en/index.html.*

Zabolotnaya, N.P., 1977, Deposits of beryllium, *in* Smirnov, V.I., ed., Ore deposits of the USSR, III: London, Pitman Publishing, p. 320–371.

Zartman, R.E., 1974, Lead isotopic provinces in the Cordillera of Western United States and their geologic significance: Economic Geology v. 69, p. 792–805.